Development and Social Justice

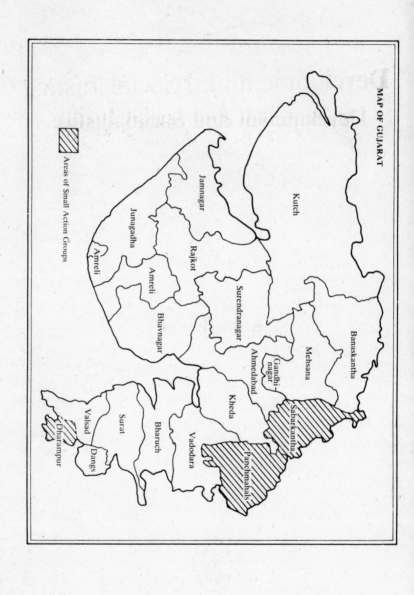

MAP OF GUJARAT

Areas of Small Action Groups

Development and Social Justice

Micro Action by Weaker Sections

ANIL BHATT

SAGE PUBLICATIONS
New Delhi/Newbury Park/London

Copyright © Anil Bhatt, 1989

First published in 1989 by
SAGE Publications India Pvt Ltd
32 M-Block Market, Greater Kailash-I
New Delhi 110 048

Sage Publications Inc  **Sage Publications Ltd**
2111 West Hillcrest Drive 28 Banner Street
Newbury Park, California 91320 London EC1Y 8QE

Published by Tejeshwar Singh for Sage Publications India Pvt Ltd, phototypeset by Mudra Typesetters, Pondicherry and printed by Chaman Offset Printers, Delhi.

Library of Congress Cataloging-in-Publication Data

Bhatt, Anil H., 1937-
    Development and social justice: micro action by weaker
sections / Anil Bhatt.
        p.   cm.
    ISBN 0–8039–9579–2 (U.S.). ISBN 0–8039–9580–6 (pbk.: U.S.)
    1. Community development—India—Citizen participation. 2. Community
organization—India. 3. Volunteer workers in community development—India.
    4. Social Justice. I. Title.
HN690. Z9C6 1986 1988
307. 1'4'0954—dc19   88–26537

ISBN 0–8039–9579–2 (US–hbk)   81–7036–115–X (India–hbk)
     0–8039–9580–6 (US–pbk)   81–7036–116–8 (India–pbk)

Contents

Frontispiece: Map of Gujarat

Foreword

For about forty years the Indian people have had an 'affair' with democracy. Of all the institutions and processes that were ushered in after (and before) Independence, it is on the democratic structure and process that the people have placed unequivocal faith, both as being exciting and liberating in itself and with a view to improving their life chances. Despite major indications that democracy is no longer what it was promised to be, that it is not proving too useful in the struggle for survival and for improving human conditions, and that it may well be producing a scenario of growing conflicts, violence and polarization in society, our faith in and positive view of the democratic process continues to this day.

In a way the Indian people have no alternative but to keep playing the democratic game; they have nothing else to fall back on in their struggles against hegemony and oppression and, with all its contradictions and disappointments, it is still the only 'hope' for the mass of the people (even though the ruling circles may not be that comfortable with the institutions of democracy which they are finding too messy, unpredictable and even dangerous for *their* survival and the privileges they happen to enjoy).

There have been two basic dimensions along which the democratic enterprise has been sought to be achieved, and in which the governing elites too believed for a long time and kept trying various methods to fulfil expectations. One of these has been the bestowing of political and social rights on the people—through the enormous span and scale of the operation of adult franchise; through competitive politics involving parties, factions and a wide array of groups; through special legislations addressed to the working classes and the 'weaker sections' and through formal and informal mechanisms of both redress of grievances and compensatory benefits to those who had for so long been the victims of history. The other has been 'development': the aim of which has been to both develop aggregate capacities for long term growth with a view to eradicating poverty and raising living standards generally and providing a fair measure of distributive justice that would remove gross inequities and injustices and move the country forward to the goal of democratic socialism. Without the second—development for achieving social justice and concretizing democratic rights—the first dimension—of party competition and electoral politics—would become vacuous and manipulative. Without the latter there can be no guarantee that development will not degenerate into managerial and technocratic dominance and the conquest of the State by a small coterie.

By the mid-sixties it became clear that neither the political nor the socio-economic dimensions of democratic transformation were, in fact, working for the people at large. It appeared that both had become privy to entrenched interests of wealth, status and power at the local, national and international levels. It also became clear that even the presumed agents of revolutionary transformation—the Left parties, the radical intellectual 'van- guards' and voluntary agencies working in rural areas that were committed to the welfare and the rights of deprived and dispos- sessed strata—had got trapped into the polarization between the privileged and the pouperized or were too engrossed in sheer games of electoral or financial kinds and had lost all sense of the larger goals. The Left is still 'progressive' in its approach to State power but this is found more in aggregate indicators of legislative and bureaucratic kinds than of a more clearly political kind that is based on the struggle for the rights of the poor and the victimized. This has, in turn, strengthened the forces of the right reaction. The result is a combination of growing alienation from the people, especially those most affected by the new structure of privilege that had been built and the deliberate neglect of these people. This neglect often borders on writing them off as too 'backward' and useless to be of any use to an elite determined to build a powerful State and emerge as a significant actor on the global scene.

Two sets of responses followed once the realization dawned that the promise of democracy and development had gone astray. Both were populist in nature but differed radically in their conceptions of populism. One was populism of *the leader* who genuinely felt that too managerial a model of the party (particularly the Congress Party) had led to a neglect of the economic dimension. In any case, she was locked in a grim battle for political ascendancy with the managerial 'syndicate'. The result was the, at once, imaginative and heady call for *garibi hatao* which steamrolled over intermediate structures and established Indira Gandhi as a supremo in direct communion with the mass of the people. The 'winning coalition', of the rural poor, the minorities and the South, that emerged did, for a while, provide hope and protection to the hitherto victimized and discriminated strata. But its main thrust was to considerably augment State power and the structures of privilege and monopoly that it embodied. It ultimately failed the 'people' and as discontent and disillusionment grew, switched over to a far worse form of a managerial model advocated by the two young Gandhis (one now deceased, the other at the helm).

The other brand of populism that emerged about the same time as *garibi hatao*, and in some ways built on its very appeal, was that of *grass-roots 'movements'*—of class, ecology, gender, ethnicity and regional and local autonomies. Some of these continued the old tradition of non-political developmental agencies of a voluntary and 'non-government' kind (of late clubbed together as NGOs). Others took much more political and partisan forms. Partisan on behalf of specific classes of people, the poor generally, the dalits, the tribals and other ethnic minorities, the women and the young, who were being subjected to all kinds of highly inimical and brutal exploitation. As the political parties began to withdraw into their electoral and exclusivist cells (exclusive vis-a-vis other parties but even more vis-a-vis dissenting elements within their own parties), and as governments became captive agents of vested interests, these new formations of a non-party political kind emerged all over. These have introduced into the democratic process a new and vibrant dimension, on the whole restricted to micro spaces, but in recent years, also seeking to align with macro associational crystallisations and larger movements like those of civil liberties and democratic rights.

As this new mode of engagement in the democratic process has grown (starting in the early seventies but really catching on during the last decade, a new set of setbacks have emerged when seen from the point of view of the worst affected strata of the population. First, the power that these grass-roots 'movement groups' are able to wield is at once marginal and fragmented. They do 'make a difference', no doubt, and have won many a victory in both protecting the oppressed from atrocities and annihilation and improving their bargaining power on things like minimum wages, compensation for displacement through loss of either land or natural environment, and safeguards against the worst forms of aggression on women. But these gains are few and scattered and more often than not dependent on either sensitive bureaucrats (or occasionally even party politicians to whom those who agree to take up this or that 'cause' have access) or the availability of middle class activists who have the skills and commitments of a progressive kind. Over time both the dependence of local populations on such 'contacts' grows and the levels of energy of the activists, harassed to no end and often 'struggling alone' and 'taking on too much'; prove unequal to either the growing repression of the State or, what is worse, cooptation by it through all kinds of allurements. Meanwhile, the much larger non-party groups and organizations of the development NGO-variety or of the 'constructive work' type that have built large empires of their own have found it 'politic' to 'keep out of politics'. The result often is that the condition of the 'wretched of the earth', has not improved substantially despite all the effort and all the clamour—investigative journalism, public interest litigation, Naxalism, new upsurges for the 'rights' of peripheral populations and communities. There is much at stake all around the old parliamentary game of elite turnovers has lost its appeal. But the danger is that the new radicalism may also produce a new set of professional politicians (alongside professional developers from the voluntary sector) who too may gradually develop their own 'constituency' and, despite the best of intentions with which they may have started, be seen as such by the people at large.

It is here that a third stream of populist awakening needs to be studied. This is the organization of the people themselves, especially of the lower castes and various tribal and marginalized peoples who have, either spontaneously or stimulated by the larger democratic currents of protest and self-determination, set up local organizations of their own. In Anil Bhatt's work we have a study of precisely this process. This, too, has its natural limitations. As and when they succeed, power struggles do emerge, 'elites' begin to bargain their way 'up' and, more often than not, the original motives and aspirations get compromized. All the same it is with this brand of people' upsurges and organizations that the future of weak and oppressed strata may lie. This study brings out where its real 'edge', over externally catalysed grass-root groupings, lies.

For detailed analyses of this—as also of the pitfalls—the reader should turn to the book proper.

May 1988   Rajni Kothari
Delhi

Preface

In 1980, the Centre for the Study of Developing Societies at Delhi initiated a rather unusual research project called Lokayan. Lokayan, which means people's movement was a project which was directly people oriented. Many people from all over the country participated in this project. The participants were activists who worked among poorer and weaker sections of society and concerned intellectuals. The methodology was that of dialogue, documentation and dissemination. The project provided scope for interaction, acquaintance and networking among organizations, groups and movements, both at the national and regional levels. A variety of people oriented issues, models, methods, techniques and technologies, ranging from ecology to exploitation, were articulated, discussed, debated and documented. It also provided an opportunity to deal with grand theories and global models of development on the one hand and local experiences and approaches at the grassroots level on the other.

I was associated with the Gujarat Unit of Lokayan. At least, in Gujarat, this project for the first time enabled various groups, agencies, activists and intellectuals to come together to discuss issues and problems of people-centred development. To the best of my knowledge it offered the first opportunity to non-established groups and activists to articulate and share their experiences.

In October 1981, one such gathering, commonly called *shibir*, was organized by the Gujarat Unit of Lokayan at Vansthali in Surat District. There, for the first time I met some poor tribal youth in their twenties and thirties with a few years of primary education, who had started small youth organizations and had undertaken in their villages some economic, developmental and social action activities. There too I met Madhusudhan Mistry, the then OXFAM Field Officer, who had been working since 1979 to encourage and support such groups managed by the rural poor themselves. I asked Mistry whether anybody had systematically evaluated these types of groups and tried to understand their efforts. As it turned out virtually nobody, including the established voluntary organizations, knew much about these youth organizations.

More than a year later, in November 1982, another *shibir* was organized jointly by Lokayan and Navyuvak Pragati Mandal, a small groups of tribals at Isri in Sabarkantha district. Many workers from several youth organizations participated. There I came to know more about these groups as they narrated their efforts and described their experiences. I spoke to Mistry about taking up a study of these groups.

Nothing came of it till the summer of 1983 when Mistry, along with Pramod Unia, approached me to undertake an evaluation of some of these groups which OXFAM was funding.

I suggested that instead of taking up an evaluation on a consulting basis as is usually done for donor agencies, which are generally narrow and mechanistic, it would be better to undertake a study with the wider purpose of understanding the small action group phenomenon.

By that time the Gujarat unit of Lokayan had been institutionalized in an organization called SETU: Centre for Knowledge and Action. I am also associated with SETU as one of the trustees. It was decided that SETU would sponsor the study for which OXFAM offered to meet all expenses. The Indian Institute of Management, Ahmedabad permitted me to undertake this study as part of my academic work at the Institute.

After preliminary discussions with Pramod Unia and Madhusudhan Mistry, I began field work in December 1983. Though originally the idea was to cover only about fifteen of the fifty-three groups OXFAM was then funding, I included more groups as I went along. I visited and met workers of forty-five of the forty-seven groups included in the list given to me by OXFAM. Of these I have included in this study thirty-eight groups on which I could gather substantial information. Because of the extensive coverage and because of my other on-going work at the Institute, I could complete the field work only in February 1985. The information and the data are primarily up to 1985 though I have included information up to 1986 wherever I could get such information.

Two earlier versions of this study, in the form of interim and final reports, were submitted to OXFAM for their internal circulation and use.

During this study Achyut Yagnik, Coordinator, Gujarat Unit of

Lokayan and Secretary, SETU, provided me with all help and support. Professor Harshad Desai edited the earlier report at considerable personal inconvenience, to meet the OXFAM deadline. Pramod Unia, who was Field Director of OXFAM when this study was initiated, showed deep understanding of my work and was flexible and liberal in negotiating the terms of the study. Barry Underwood, his successor, was also helpful. Madhusudhan Mistry, helped me patiently in working out the logistics, putting me in touch with groups and facilitating my work in many other ways. We had innumerable discussions in different places and at odd hours. He gave freely of his knowledge, information and insight in a true collaborative spirit.

In the first couple of field visits I was accompanied by Bhanubhai Adhvaryu, a school teacher, freedom fighter and activist who relentlessly fought for the poor. He was the founder of Shramjivi Samaj, an organization of the poor created as a sequal to a land-grab movement which he successfully led. Unfortunately, he fell ill soon after and passed away.

Ashok Shrimali assisted me in this study right from the beginning. He accompanied me on field visits and looked after all arrangements. He took copious notes and helped in preparing field reports. My secretary, Ravi Kumar, put up with my rather anarchic ways of working with patience and understanding. He typed several drafts of this study. The report version of the study which had to meet a deadline required him to work on weekends, at night and right into the early hours of the morning. My friend, Harsh Sethi, of Lokayan read through the draft and made valuable suggestions.

My wife Nila and children Bijal and Saket have, with love and understanding, supported my frequent and long periods of absence from home during field work, and seclusion even while at home. They ungrudgingly allowed our home to be used for conducting interviews for this study and warmly welcomed many friends from small groups, OXFAM and SETU.

May 1988   Anil Bhatt
Ahmedabad.

1

Introduction: Macro Perspectives of Micro Action

In the last two decades much attention has been paid to grass-roots organizations, programmes and movements for development and justice, independent of established government and political organizations.

These grass-roots efforts are many and varied in size, approach, strategy, and ideology. Perhaps the one thing common to all is that they are formally independent of government (though many collaborate with or take funds from government) and political parties (though some indirectly support political groups or individual politicians).

This phenomenon of grass-roots action through independent, small (though size varies considerably) groups is also described as micro movements or action, voluntarism and non-party political process, depending upon the framework of analysis.

Mostly young, middle class, generally highly educated, concerned and committed people have turned to these grass-roots activities, instead of joining government or political parties as one would have normally expected of those who wanted to do public work.

This is because there has been an increasing realization since the late sixties and particularly after the emergency in the mid-seventies, that conventional governmental programmes, political institutions and political organizations have failed to reduce poverty, inequality and injustice.

While government has launched and attempted to implement many development programmes with many different structures, institutions and designs, it has failed to make any noticeable impact on poverty, inequality and injustice.[1]

---

[1] Virtually every study and evaluation of government programmes of development done by outsiders and some done by the government itself have pointed this

By the mid-seventies it had become clear that attempts at development through numerous official programmes had barely touched the poor, the marginal and weaker sections of society, let alone change the social order marked by exploitation and oppression of the poor and the weak.

The massive and comprehensive community development programmes of the fifties which were incorporated into the panchayati raj system by the early sixties had not made any noticeable dent. All accounts of both the systems were highly critical and generally negative.

As all accounts revealed that poverty was increasing and even the trickle-down effect that was predicted did not take place, a new target group oriented approach was developed in the seventies. The mid-seventies saw a spate of such programmes and schemes. This approach was developed because of the realization that if the poor are to be helped, special and concerted efforts will have to be made to reach them through separate and exclusive programmes.

The decade of the seventies saw a mushrooming of such programmes, projects and schemes; and also agencies and organizations. Tribal Development Plans, Tribal Development Corporations, Rural Development Corporations, Small Farmers' Development Agencies, Marginal Farmers' and Agricultural Labourers' Programmes, Antyodaya and Sarvodaya schemes, Food-for-Work Programmes, Integrated Rural Development Programmes, National Rural Employment Programme were some of the more well-known programmes. Besides, many non-economic programmes not exclusively meant for the poor, but poor-oriented in their design, content and intent, were also launched. National Adult Education Programme and Maternity, Child Health and Nutrition Schemes were started.

Along with the target group approach strong impetus was given to decentralized planning. Exercises in block level planning, with the help of research institutions and non-government organizations working in the field, were undertaken.

---

out repeatedly. There is vast literature on this but for the latest and somewhat more comprehensive review see, L C Jain et al, *Grass Without Roots: Rural Development Under Government Auspices*, New Delhi: Sage, 1985. Also see for an overall review Anil Bhatt, 'Social & Political Dimensions of Administering Development,' in John Ickis et al (eds.), *Beyond Bureaucracy*, West Hartford, USA: Kumarian Press, 1987.

Attempts were also made to improve field level administration. The departmental form of organization and administration was increasingly being discarded in favour of agencies, boards, commissions, cooperatives, corporations and project administrations. Many minor and frequent changes in powers, functions and other administrative arrangements of the district administration were also made.

In spite of all this the delivery system, as the development administration has come to be called at the operational level, has proved far too weak and ineffective to reach the poor.

The development administration has faced powerful social and political barriers at local levels in reaching the poor. Since the local elite and dominant groups have vested interests in perpetuating the deprivation, they block and even violently oppose any attempts at improvement of these groups. Local institutions like rural banks, cooperative societies, panchayati raj institutions, are dominated by these elites. The bureaucracy in charge of delivery of services to the poor is also dominated by them and dependent on them. So the benefits to be derived from these institutions, schemes, projects and programmes are siphoned off by entrenched interests. Paradoxically, a more effective and efficient delivery of services to the poor would require greater decentralization: more powers, resources and participatory opportunities at lower levels. But in the social and political context of rural India, the greater the decentralization the higher the possibility of such power, resources and participation being centralized in the hands of the powerful few at the local level, helping to tighten the grip of the dominant over the deprived.[2]

Thus the decade of the sixties and seventies have seen a wide and bewildering variety of projects, programmes and schemes of development. There have been numerous and frequent changes in administration and administrative arrangements. And yet the poor have not benefited.

The open competitive political process on which some had pinned so much faith during the sixties in the hope that the franchise, the

[2] See Anil Bhatt, 'Decentralization for Rural Development: An Overview of South Asian Experiences' and 'Making Decentralization Work for the Poor,' in Anil Bhatt et al., *Building From Below: Local Initiatives for Decentralized Development in Asia and Pacific*, Kuala Lumpur, Malaysia: Asian and Pacific Development Centre. Vols. I & II, 1987.

elections and the compulsions of market mechanisms of competitive politics would result in a shift of power and influence to the
people at the bottom, has been belied.[3] Political action, whether
by government or opposition, was not only proving ineffective in
helping the benefits of development to go to the poor, but was
even impeding the process and instead helping entrenched sections
to capture benefits specifically meant for the poor. With the decline
of democratic norms and procedures at higher levels of politics,
and the consequent weakening of government and its authority,
politics became increasingly brutalized and lumpenized. By the
early eighties entrenched interests, emboldened by the weakening
of authority of the state and insecurity of higher political leadership, had mounted open and brutal counter-offensives to attempts
at emancipation of the weak, down-trodden and the poor.
Economic exploitation was backed up by physical oppression.

The traditional political organizations at macro level, even those
claiming to be specifically working for the lower classes such as
kisan sabhas, trade unions and leftist political parties, have been
largely ineffective. As Harsh Sethi has argued, the more conventional and larger political organizations like political parties and
their mass-fronts are, 'unscrupulous, unprincipled, corrupt,
bureaucratic and vanguardist.'[4] Even the revolutionary parties,
argues Rajni Kothari, 'have been contained and in part coopted, .
. . that there is a growing hiatus between these parties and lower
classes.'[5]

In the face of the failure of government and conventional governmental and political institutions, small scale initiatives at the
grass-roots level, it is argued, would provide a political but non-
partisan alternative. These initiatives are seen as based on

> deep stirrings of consciousness . . . that could be turned into a
> catalyst of new opportunity. It is to be seen as a response to the
> incapacity of the state to hold its various constituents in a

---

[3] See Rajni Kothari, *Politics in India*, Boston: Little Brown & Co., 1970.

[4] Harsh Sethi, 'Elements of a Collective Autobiography' in his 'The Non-party
Political Process: Uncertain Alternatives,' Delhi: UNRISD/Lokayan, mimeo.,
1983. Also see, his 'Groups in a New Politics of Transformation' *Economic &
Political Weekly*, Vol. XIX, No. 7, 18 Feb. 1984.

[5] Rajni Kothari, 'The Non-Party Political Process,' *EPW*, Vol. XIX, No. 5, 4
Feb. 1984.

framework of positive action . . . as attempts to open alternative political spaces outside the usual arenas of party and government though not outside the state.[6]

These grass-root organizations and movements attempt to redefine politics as something different and beyond electoral and legislative politics; and also redefine it in terms of its content by widening the arena of politics to include such subjects as health, rights over forests and community resources, ecological, cultural and educational issues.[7] These initiatives have 'potential to blossom into a macro movement for alternative development.'[8]

Attention is increasingly being given to these independent micro action groups also because the traditional macro organizations have failed to bring about any effective development or social transformation in spite of all the resources that they command and have consumed in the last four decades. Sethi argues that

the traditional macro organizations suffer not only from rigid, hierarchical and bureaucratic structures, making an innovative and flexible approach difficult, if not impossible, they seem blessed with the most egoistical attitude with respect to their own infallibility.[9]

Indeed they have decayed and degenerated to a level where any change through established channels, like elections or reforms, seem remote.

There is still a third reason why such grass-roots level small efforts need to be paid careful attention. Purely in developmental and apparently nonpolitical terms but with pro-poor and pro-people perspectives they provide critiques and alternatives to strategies, approaches, activities, designs and programmes of development through government and the organized non-governmental establishments such as those of doctors, engineers, the corporate sector and international aid-giving organizations. Based on their small but grass-roots experiments and experiences they

[6] *Ibid.*
[7] Ibid. D L Sheth, 'Grass-roots Initiatives in India,' *EPW*, Vol. XIX, No. 6, 11 Feb. 1984.
[8] D L Sheth, *ibid.*
[9] Harsh Sethi, 'Groups in a New Politics of Transformation,' *op. cit.*

provide powerful critiques of the healthcare systems; social forestry; big dams, water and wasteland development programmes; forest policies; drug policies; dangers of eucalyptus plantation, chemical fertilizers; corporate interest and activities in rural development. They further attempt to develop concrete alternatives to the traditional healthcare system; provide information on such diverse matters as medicines and how to get them at a low cost, irrigation projects, tree plantations for afforestation; and even define the role of hawkers in the urban economy. They have pioneered new and untried approaches to development and contributed to the knowledge on development.[10] They help demystify the technical, the professional and the big. Their work has helped considerably in introducing 'people orientation' rather than only professional and technical orientations in big development projects and schemes. Even powerful professional establishments have to often take note of their observations and halt or modify their programmes, activities and approaches accordingly.[11]

In specific developmental terms too the work of these small organizations is getting increasing attention. Though governmental attempts have failed to bring about development in spite of nearly four decades of massive and varied efforts, these small organizations seem to be successful and effective in income generation and agricultural developmental activities; development of natural resources such as water, land, trees and forests; and improving the health and level of education of the rural poor.

United Nation's agencies, international and foreign-funding agencies—both governmental and voluntary, international research institutes and even management institutions which till recently confined their attention to industry and government, are all paying increasing attention to these small independent action groups, popularly known as non-governmental organizations. International

---

[10] See Terry Alliband, *Catalysts of Development*, USA, West Hartford: Kumarian Press, 1983; Claude Alvares, 'Deadly Development,' *Development Forum* 11: 3, Oct. 1983; Anil Sadagopal, 'Between Question and Clarity: What is the role of Science?' *Science Today*, Oct. 1981; Shashi Pandey, 'Role of Voluntary Action in Rural India,' *South Asia Bulletin*, 4: 2, Fall, 1984.

[11] The Government of India Forest Bill of 1980 is a good example. Voluntary action groups particularly working among tribals and concerned with ecology protested actively against the bill. Several meetings, rallies, workshops were organized and ultimately the Government had to postpone the passage of the bill into Act. See, Walter Fernandes and Sharad Kulkarni (eds.), *Towards a New Forest Policy*, Delhi: Indian Social Institute, 1983.

organizations, funding agencies and their expatriate representatives and consultants, generally look for success stories for replication.[12] Hence the emphasis on evaluations and case studies of successful non-governmental organizations.

Those who look for development through independent small organizations, instead of development through government alone, feel that because these voluntary efforts are small, on the ground and backed by greater commitment and concern for the poor and deprived, they are more effective in bringing about development. The major emphasis in this view is laid on the participation of the poor in developmental activities which will raise their skills, confidence and self-esteem and eventually lead to self-reliance so that they are able to manage their own development.[13] The basic argument is somewhat like this: the governments of developing countries have largely failed to take the benefits of development to the poor and also failed to contain and curtail vested interests who oppress and exploit the poor and appropriate the maximum benefits of government sponsored and managed development. The poor therefore must mobilize and organize themselves so that they become powerful enough to reach up and pull down to them the benefits of development.

This approach does not directly and explicitly challenge the existing political system and its political, economic and adminis-

---

[12] United Nations agencies—UNDP, FAO, WHO, ILO—have all launched studies, activities and programmes for NGOs and grass-roots level small organizations. Government of India has specific allocations for these groups in the seventh plan and an explicit policy of collaborating with NGOs. The formation of the Council of People's Action and Rural Technology (CAPART) by the Government of India is but one example. International research organizations like UNRISD in Geneva and APDC in Kuala Lumpur also focus their research more and more on NGOs, farmers and people's organizations and people's initiatives and participation in development. Management institutions in the country have also entered the field by undertaking studies, consultancies and conferences. There is even an international group called 'Management Institutes' Working Group on Social Development.'

[13] There are scores of studies and documents and even some institutions solely to look into participatory approaches for development and self-reliance. For illustrative examples see, Mohd. Anisur Rahmad (ed.), *Grass-roots Participation and Self-Reliance*, New Delhi: Oxford IBH, 1984. CVS D'Silva et al. 'Bhoomi Sena: A Struggle for People's Power,' *Development Dialogue*, 1979:2. Ravi J. Matthai, *The Rural University: The Jawaja Experiment in Educational Innovations*, Bombay: Popular Prakashan, 1985. V. Paranjape et al, *Grass-roots Self-Reliance in Shramik Sanghtna*, Geneva: ILO, Working Paper 10/WQ22, 1981.

trative institutions. But it increasingly pins faith on smaller local initiatives and efforts for development. It is concerned with participation and its various components: who participates, how far, the types and levels of participation, mechanisms and process of participation. This view focusses on participation of people in their own development, not so much because it would lead to the radical and rapid transformation of the political system and its processes, but because it would lead to more direct and immediate development—rise in income and production, development of infrastructure, improvement in health and education etc. The concern lies largely with what one may broadly call managerial dimensions of these small, local level organizations.

This approach generally looks at the genesis, leadership, forms and structure of organization, identification of activities and selection of technologies, programme designs, entry points, strategies and tactics, types and methods of training, funds and costs, types and levels of participation, achievements and performance and monitoring and evaluation. If such organizations or their projects and programmes are successful then interest in replication, extension and scaling up is generated.

Some variants of the communist political groupings though, have strongly criticized this small action group phenomenon and its theoretical formulations that view the role of these groups and movements as major non-party non-government alternatives for development and social transformation. They see in these independent actions groups of different varieties, including struggle-oriented and militant groups, the imperialist conspiracy of capitalist powers to counter the revolution and revolutionary forces. Their argument is briefly as follows: the imperialist powers have realized that the governments of the third world have failed to ensure any reforms and initiate development. The ruling classes, vested interests and the bureaucracy are narrow, elitist and short-sighted and therefore they have not taken minimum measures like land reforms to narrow the widening disparities which create socially explosive situations. That is why they have developed this new strategy—subtle, sophisticated and sinister—in which they circumvent the governments and other oligarchic establishments to directly support and fund voluntary organizations working at the grassroots level.

While the aid to official agencies will continue another pipeline must be opened which has direct access to people. The political fall-out of this strategy will help to avoid the danger of the poverty-striken masses falling prey to subversive revolutionary movements which would abort the process of capitalist development.

Indian theorists of this voluntary action and activists working at the grass-roots are willy-nilly aiding and abetting this imperialist strategy with these 'eclectic and pseudo-radical postures . . . . For how else one can explain the strange spectacle of imperialist agencies and governments funding organizations to organize the rural and urban poor to fight for their rights and against exploitation.'[14]

It should also be noted, however, that some very radical groups with revolutionary ideology who strive for fundamental changes in the social, political and economic order in the country, and who are against developmental voluntary organization and foreign funding of these efforts, are also actively involved in working in specified small areas taking up local issues for struggle, instead of working for a nation-wide revolutionary movement through large party organizations. A short while ago I attended a gathering of small action group activists where Mahendra Chaudhary of the Rajasthan Kisan Sangathan argued that no small voluntary organization can carry on a struggle and development simultaneously. But he also argued in favour of working at local levels in small groups, taking up local issues for struggle, at least initially. His view point was to work at local levels, taking up local issues of exploitation and injustice and continuously, repeatedly and relentlessly pointing out to the people the exploitative and oppressive social and political system. People should be involved in these struggles dealing with their own local and immediate issues. This would bring about *jagruti* (awakening) and *chetna* (consciousness). Once the poor and the deprived are thus aroused others would join leading to a macro-movement. But one must start with the small, the local and from the bottom.

[14] The strongest and most organized public statements of this view is given by Prakash Karat of CPI(M) in his 'Action-Groups/Voluntary Agencies: A Factor in Imperialist Strategy,' *The Marxist*, Apr–June 1984. The summary of this viewpoint and the quotes given here are from this paper. For a retort to this article see Harsh Sethi, 'The Immoral Others: The Debate between Party and Non-Party Groups,' *EPW*, Vol. XX, No. 9, 2 March 1985.

In sum, the role that these small grass-roots level independent groups and movements are seen to be performing are broadly of the following types:

1. Development of the poor, weak and oppressed in specified local areas in any one or more of development sectors such as agriculture, health, education etc.
2. Experimentation and innovation in approaches, models, techniques, strategies and developmental activities. And to thus provide inputs, critiques and alternatives to the existing approaches, models, techniques, and policies.
3. Bringing pressures; and influencing laws, legislations, policies, programmes and projects; in favour of the poor.
4. To bring about social transformation, change the political and economic systems and their institutions and establishments, such that the very basic structure of domination and deprivation, inequalities and injustice would collapse and a new and just social and political order would emerge. As per at least one view discussed above, these groups may play precisely the opposite role: that of preventing or delaying the fundamental transformation.

Basically, there are two operational ideologies—harmony and conflict—with which the small groups attempt to perform these roles. These are also referred to as developmental versus struggle approaches. In the harmony approach the emphasis is more on working for the concrete development of the poor with the assumption that appropriate management, appropriate technology, and idealism (of helping the poor) are the critical elements that can deliver the goods. Development of the poor is here believed to be possible without politics and without any reference to the power holders. Collaboration with government, industry, rich people and institutions of the establishment are permissible.

In the conflict approach it is believed the root cause of the poverty and exploitation is the power structure of society and therefore what is needed is to mobilize and organize the poor to fight against established power holders: be they landlords, money-lenders, traders, bureaucrats, politicians or government itself. Such movements and organizations work among the poor to bring about awareness and organize them at local levels to fight against corruption, injustice or exploitation. They use direct action methods more often. These methods may include preparation and distribution of pamphlets and petitions, meetings, rallies, gheraos, sit-ins, land grab etc.

To be sure one may find mixes of these approaches in varying degrees in a single group or movement. But in all these different ways of looking at these small independent groups one thing is clear. They are seen as an alternative to what one may now call conventional and traditional—though only forty years old—ways of development through established governmental and political channels.

Whether the interest is social or political transformation or effective management of development and whether the approach is one of harmony or conflict, the emphasis is on small independent groups at the grass-roots.

In what follows I have attempted to analyze from these different perspectives a rather unusual phenomenon of small action groups of weaker sections in Gujarat, a western Indian state.

As mentioned earlier there is tremendous variety in what are called small groups and differently referred to as grass-roots initiatives, voluntary organizations, non-governmental organizations, micro movements and so on. The variety and overlap in terms of size, activities, approaches, strategies, styles and ideologies defy any neat and comprehensive categorization or classification.[15] 'At a formal level,' says Harsh Sethi, 'the only common characteristic of such organizations is that they are registered under the Societies Registration Act, are not expected to make any profit on their activities and are considered non-governmental.'[16] However, most of these groups, movements and activities are organized and led by urbanized and educated people who out of agony at the state of affairs, altruism or commitment, decided to work for development, or fight on behalf of the poor, or both. To this extent these are led and managed by 'outsiders.' That is, the main initiators, leaders, catalysts, change-agents or animators do not belong socially, culturally or economically to the communities of the people for or with whom they work. The issues and activities that they take up

[15] For some attempts at categorization, see Harsh Sethi, 'Groups in a New Politics of Transformation,' *op. cit.* and Shashi Pandey 'Role of Voluntary Action in Rural India,' *South Asia Bulletin*, Vol. IV, No. 2, Fall 1984.

[16] Sethi, *ibid.*

are not primarily their's nor the problems they fight for are their personal problems. Sethi in attempting a description states that 'these groups are organizations composed mainly of sensitized or radicalized middle class youth, working for and with the oppressed and exploited strata with a view to transform society.'[17]

In case of the outsiders, self-reliance and independence of the people they work for, the question of their withdrawal and the continuity and longetivity of their organizations and activities, crop up regularly and inevitably.

In contrast, the groups studied here are entirely manned and managed by weaker sections with minimal outside intervention and with very small amounts of outside funding. Some of these groups came up spontaneously without any outside stimulation; others were formed as a result of the example set by already existing groups in the neighbouring villages; while still others were formed as a result of persuasion, stimulation and help provided by some existing groups.

Many groups led and managed by outsiders involve the poor people with varying degrees of participation and involvement. Some of these outsiders claim to work only as catalysts or animators. Yet in reality they play a pivotal role. They stimulate, give ideas, provide strategies, bring information and funds. Even in the process of dialogues and discussions, which are often claimed to be mechanisms for people's participation in decision-making, there are subtle and sometimes not so subtle ways in which hints and ideas provided by outside catalysts influence the thinking of the groups.

This is not in any way to criticize the participatory or decision-making processes or to argue that there is anything particularly wrong in outsiders being involved in working for the poor; but to underline the fact that the role of outsiders, even as catalysts and even in those cases where the primary objective is mobilization, organization and conscientization of the poor, remains primary and central.

It is also to underline the difference between grass-roots groups on which so much attention has been directed recently and the grass-roots groups which I am going to discuss.

While discussing these groups I shall discuss their genesis, their

[17] Sethi, *ibid.*

membership and leadership, their organizations, their interaction with the outside world, their activities and implications of their activities. Finally, I shall also attempt to discuss this rather unusual phenomenon of small action groups of weaker sections against the larger perspective of the role of micro action in development and social transformation.

2

The Groups and the Study

The groups discussed here are called small because many of them had their activities confined to one village. Some of the groups covered more than one village but their activities rarely extended beyond eight or ten villages and even in these cases they were most active only in one or two villages. Their formal membership ranged between a minimum of twenty-one to a maximum of 250 and out of the thirty-eight groups studied here as many as twelve groups had membership below fifty.

They are action groups because they have taken up economic, educational, social justice, social reform and conscientization activities. They are groups because although there is a formal structure (office holders, executive committee, membership, constitution etc.), and they are all officially registered with the Charity Commissioner or with the Registrar of Cooperative Societies, their activities extend beyond their formal structure and their methods of operation are more in the nature of groups than highly structured organizations. Moreover, they also cater to those members of the community who are not formally their members. The active members of the groups (mostly executive committee members and office holders) often involve themselves singly or in twos and threes in issues and events in the community which are not formally within the purview of the group or officially taken up as group activities though recognized and considered as such. Barring economic and formal developmental activities their other developmental, social justice, social reform, advisory, facilitative, catalystic activities or political interventions in the communities are unstructured and at best only loosely organized. It is for these reasons that it would be more appropriate to view them as groups rather than organizations.

Barring some cooperative societies, all other groups are called mandals: a Gujarati term which I think very aptly conveys the nature of their organization which is not highly structured in terms of specified roles and activities for its leaders and members and not hierarchical in nature. Therefore, throughout this study they are referred to as mandals or groups.

All the groups are manned and managed by tribals, scheduled castes or other backward castes like Thakardas, Koli Bariyas (Baxi Panch castes)[1] or Thuris, a nomadic tribe. While some of the groups have salary-earning and relatively better off leaders, all the mandals cater to economically and socially weaker sections.

All the groups, barring one which is a cooperative society of labourers in construction work, are in rural areas and all but two are in predominantly backward areas of Gujarat. As shown in the map of Gujarat they are in the eastern belt which is hilly, forested, generally drought prone, officially declared backward and wholly or predominantly tribal. The groups are in Dharampur Taluka of Valsad District, in Dangs District in Southern Gujarat, in Panch-mahals District and in Sabarkantha District. Dharampur and Dangs are almost exclusively tribal areas. Panchmahals and Sabarkantha are also substantially tribal districts. Barring Ahmedabad District, all the areas in which these mandals are established are officially declared as backward areas.

At the last count in July 1984 (the number seems to be increasing with every count) there were 180 groups including cooperative societies.[2] The district-wise break up is given below in Table 1. This table was prepared following inquiries among the people. The table does not include every group in existence such as some mandals which are not registered but have been in operation for one to three years and are involved in economic and other activities. The thirty-eight mandals included in the study have a total membership of over 2,500 and their activities cover a population of approximately 82,000.

The great majority of active workers—office bearers and executive committee members—are young, almost all below forty. There is only one mandal whose president is fifty-two. There are several mandals whose leaders are in their early thirties and three of the

---

[1] A Commission appointed by the Government of Gujarat under the Chairman-ship of Justice Baxi, prepared a schedule of eighty socially and economically backward castes and non-Hindu groups other than scheduled castes and tribes. These are popularly known as Baxi Panch castes.

[2] By the beginning of 1986 the number of mandals had gone up to at least 230.

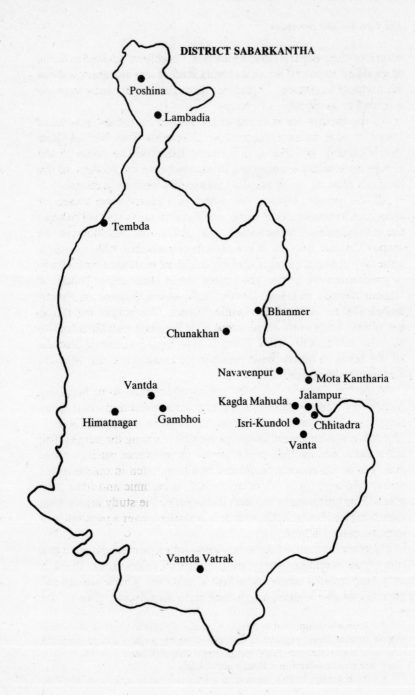

DISTRICT SABARKANTHA

- Poshina
- Lambadia
- Tembda
- Bhanmer
- Chunakhan
- Navavenpur
- Mota Kantharia
- Vantda
- Kagda Mahuda
- Jalampur
- Himatnagar
- Gambhoi
- Isri-Kundol
- Chhitadra
- Vanta
- Vantda Vatrak

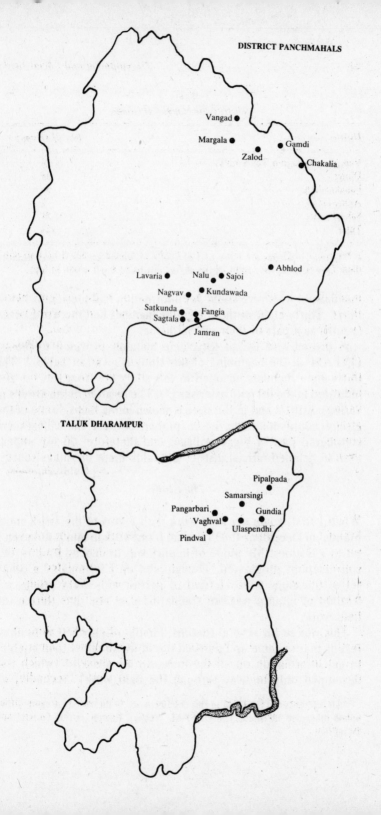

DISTRICT PANCHMAHALS

Vangad

Margala
Gamdi
Zalod
Chakalia

Abhlod

Lavaria   Nalu Sajoi
Nagvav   Kundawada
Satkunda   Fangia
Sagtala
Jamran

TALUK DHARAMPUR

Pipalpada
Samarsingi
Pangarbari   Gundia
Vaghval   Ulaspendhi
Pindval

TABLE 1
Districtwise Number of Groups

District	No. of Groups
Valsad (Dharampur Taluk only)	18
Dangs*	38
Panchmahals	50
Ahmedabad	2
Sabarkantha	21
Total	124

* Groups in Dangs are not a part of OXFAM funded groups. I have included them here because they fulfil all the characteristics of small action groups.

mandals on which we could get information had presidents below thirty. Thirty-eight of the forty-nine mandals had the word *yuvak* (youth) as a part of their official name.

A district-wise list of forty-nine mandals provided to me by OXFAM[3] at the beginning of this study is given in Table 2. The thirty-eight mandals included in this study are from this list and indicated in the list with asterisks (*). The location of the groups in various districts and in the state is shown in the maps. Some of the groups could not however be plotted because the villages are considered part of bigger villages and therefore, do not appear even in detailed official district and taluk maps or village census.

The Study

When I first began my field work with a visit to the Isri-Kundol Mandal in December 1983 I had no framework in mind; not even a set of questions. My mode of inquiry was to depend on how our conversations progressed. Though later on I formulated a rough set of questions which I tried to persue with every group, my method of inquiry was not standardized at any time during the field work.

This was so for several reasons. Firstly, often when some interesting matter came up I persued this in-depth rather than attempt to get information on all the items on my checklist (which was developed only midway through the field work). Secondly, all

[3] All references to OXFAM in this document are to its Western Region Office unless otherwise specified. The OXFAM, Western Region, covers Gujarat and Rajasthan.

TABLE 2
List of Groups

A. District: Sabarkantha

Taluk: Khedbrahma
1.* New Pragati Yuvak Mandal, Poshina.
2.* Adarsh Pragati Yuvak Mandal, Lambadia.
3.* Tembda Piyat Sahakari Mandali Ltd., Tembda.

Taluk: Bhiloda
4.* Arunodaya Yuva Vartul, Chunakhan.
5. Bhanmer Piyat Sahakari Mandali Ltd., Bhanmer.
6.* Adivasi Pragati Mandal, Navavenpur.
7.* Shri Navyuvak Pragati Mandal, Isri-Kundol.
8.* Subhash Yuvak Mandal, Kagda Mahuda.
9.* Navful Yuvak Mandal, Mota Kantharia.
10.* Shri Kasturba Mahila Mandal, Isri-Kundol.

Taluk: Himatnagar
11.* Vantda Dudh Utpadak Sahakari Mandali Ltd., Vantda.
12.* Himatnagar Taluk Vanskamdar Sahakari Mandali Ltd., Gambhoi.
13. Sabar Yuva Vikas Mandal, C/o Nehru Yuvak Kendra, Himatnagar.

Taluk: Bayad
14.* Vantda-Vatrak Vanskamdar Sahakari Mandali Ltd. Vantda-Vatrak.

Taluk: Meghraj
15.* Vanvasi Gram Vikas Mandal, Vanta.
16.* Gandhi Pragati Yuvak Mandal, Jalampur.
17.* Shri Pragati Mandal, Chitadra.

B. District: Panchmahals

Taluk: Santrampur
18.* Jaijawan Jai Kissan Adivasi Sarvodaya Yuvak Mandal, Margala.
19.* Vangad Yuvak Mandal, Vangad.
20. Adivasi Mahila Pragati Mandal (Santrampur Vibhag), Vangad.

Taluk: Zalod
21.* Panchmahals Jilla Adivasi Samaj Kalyan Yuvak Mandal, Zalod.
22.* Gamdi Vibhag Yuvak Mandal, Gamdi.
23. Chakalia Vibhag Yuvak Mandal, Chakalia.

Taluk: Limkheda
24. Adivasi Mahila Jagruti Mandal (Sajoi Vibhag), Sajoi.
25. Vibhagiya Yuvak Mandal Nalu, Nalu.
26.* Kundawada Vibhag Adivasi Yuvak Mandal, Kundawada.

Taluk: Dahod
27.* Abhlod Yuvak Mandal, Abhlod.

Taluk: Devgadh Baria
28.* Lavaria Vibhag Adivasi Yuvak Mandal, Lavaria.

29. Laxmi Dudh Utpadak Sahakari Mandali, Sagtala.
30.* Satkunda Grahak Bhandar, Satkunda.
31.* Jamran Vibhag Adivasi Yuvak Mandal, Jamran.
32.* Nagvav Vibhag Adivasi Yuvak Mandal, Nagvav.
33. Mahila Jagriti Mandal Fangia Vibhag, Fangia.
34. Fangia Gram Laxmi Dudh Utpadak Mandali, Fangia.
35.* Mithibor Vibhag Adivasi Yuvak Mandal, Mithibor.

C. District: Valsad

Taluk: Dharampur
36.* Shri Datt Samuhik Adivasi Yuvak Mandal, Vaghval.
37.* Shri Bajrangbali Adivasi Yuva Mandal, Ulaspendi.
38.* Shri Chetana Adivasi Yuvak Mandal, Gundia.
39.* Shri Navsarjan Yuvak Mandal, Pangarbari.
40.* Shri Ramakrishna Adivasi Yuvak Mandal, Samarsingi.
41.* Gupteshwar Adivasi Yuvak Mandal, Pindwal.
42.* Shri Ghyaneshvar Adivasi Yuvak Mandal, Mordanad.
43.* Shri Pangarbari Gundia Adivasi Yuvak Mandal, Pangarbari.
44.* Shri Bhadrakali Adivasi Yuvak Mandal, Tamchadi.
45.* Shri Keshrinandan Adivasi Yuvak Mandal, Koshimpada.
46.* Shri Gupteshwar Adivasi Yuvak Mandal, Dhamni.
47.* Shri Rameshwar Adivasi Yuvak Mandal, Pipalpada.

D. District: Ahmedabad

Taluk: Daskoi
48. Rojka Harijan Khetmajoor Sahakari Mandali Ltd., Rojka.
49. Viswakarma Bhandhkam Majoor Sahakari Mandali Ltd., Ahmedabad.

mandals did not have the information that I needed. Some mandals like Poshina, Gamdi or Abhlod kept very detailed, accurate and systematic records; others like Mithibor or Jamran had hardly any records. With some mandals I spent a long time while with others hardly a day was spent. I could meet a great many members of some mandals while in others I could meet only two or three. Information was collected from OXFAM records and from conversations and in-depth interviews with Mistry, the Oxfam Field Officer, and with some leaders of mandals who even supplied a lot of information about other mandals. Data was gathered from records of mandals. In-depth interviews of leaders and members of these mandals were held in their villages, in the various *shibirs* (training camps) held for these mandals at various places, and at my home in Ahmedabad whenever any mandal people happened to visit Ahmedabad. I interviewed people from all the established voluntary organizations working in the areas of the mandals to know their views on the mandals.

My approach in this study has not been purely academic and clinical. I must state at the outset that my sympathies and support are with these groups and I would like to see them develop and become stronger. During the field work, therefore, I have not merely acted as a detached investigator whose only function is to gather correct and accurate information. I have given them information, pointed out limitations and dangers of their strategy, suggested alternatives and often entered into arguments with them. During the field work if they come up with some major problem in thier work I spent most of the time discussing it and left the place with very little information for my checklist.

During the field work, while participating in *shibirs*, talking about these groups informally to other friends and formally in seminars and conferences and while writing the earlier versions of this document, my own emotional pendulum has swung back and forth from exhilaration to depression.

Originally when I started the field work I was given a list of forty-nine groups by OXFAM. It was expected and I too had thought that I would study about ten or twelve groups of different types or having different characteristics. But after I started I was drawn to look into as many mandals as possible. Thus, instead of only doing detailed case studies of a few selected mandals—though I have done that too—I decided to look into as many mandals as possible even though it sometimes meant not getting enough details about each mandal.

Covering as many groups as possible also meant that I had to forego collecting detailed information of the kind generally included in standard social science research, such as information about villages, tribal culture and customs and tribal stratification, unless when it directly reflected on the work and character of the mandals.

I have used examples, incidents and events. I have used quantities wherever it was possible. Some of the tables are based on my assessment and therefore are judgemental. I have presented four case studies to give a more detailed and concrete idea about the mandals. I have adopted this mix because, given the varied and uneven sources of information and a wide variation among the groups, I have found this to be the most effective way of giving a comprehensive view of the multi-dimensionality of this small group phenomenon. This study, therefore, may not prove to be a methodologist's delight nor an activist's manual. It is a mix of quantitative and qualitative data, of description, analysis, observation and suggestion.

Appendix I

A Note on the Governmental and Socio-Economic Context of the Groups

The structure of local government, politics and public institutions is very large, elaborate and complicated in rural Gujarat. One can easily get confused with the variety and complexity of positions, levels and terms. A contextual brief note is given here for those who are not familiar with the governmental and socio-economic structure of the areas in which these groups operate.

In Gujarat there is a three tier system of rural local government popularly called panchayati raj. The basic unit is the gram (village) panchayat. It is an elected body based on universal adult franchise. In the case of small villages, there is a group panchayat where three to five villages are grouped together. Many of the villages in which small groups are working, are part of a group panchayat, and therefore not even listed in census reports or shown in official district and taluk maps.

The head of the village panchayat is called *sarpanch*, who is directly elected. The village panchayat, depending on the size of the village, has between nine to thirteen elected members called *panchs*. At the village level, the revenue clerk called *talati* works as a secretary of the village panchayat. He is in charge of all land records and deals with land revenue. He is also responsible to the revenue department headed by a *mamlatdar*, an important revenue and judicial officer at the taluk level.

Besides, the district collector appoints a member of the community as a police patel. Before independence the police patel or *mukhi* (headman) as he is called, occupied by heredity a very important and powerful position. He was the only member of the community linked officially with the government during the British Raj and along with the *talati* looked after land revenue, land records, law and order and all public matters related to his village. Now the *mukhi* is appointed and is supposed to assist the police in law and order work. The *mukhi, talati* and now the *sarpanch* are the most powerful village elite representing public authorities and are generally notorious for their corruption, exploitation and oppression of the villagers.

Several departments or programmes have functionaries looking after a group of four, five or ten villages and known by a variety of different names. Usually the Taluk Development Office has a functionary called village level worker (VLW). The agricultural department has extension workers looking after several villages. The National Adult Education Programme has sector supervisors looking after thirty adult education centres and depending upon the number of centres in a village the jurisdiction may range from ten to twenty-five villages. The Primary Health Centres (PHC) at the Taluk level have health supervisors who generally look after a population of 20,000. The PHC also has sub-centres with Auxiliary Nurse Midwife (ANM) looking after a population of 10,000; and 5,000 in case of some special project districts like Panchmahals. All these functionaries are usually supposed to stay within their allotted areas but most do not do so, particularly in tribal areas.

Several village panchayats form a taluk panchayat. This body called panchayat samiti consists of representatives of village panchayats and a few coopted members. The presidentship of a Taluk panchayat is a political position. It is at this level that political parties officially put forward their candidates for election as president and chairman of various committees of the taluk panchayat.

The administrative side of the taluk panchayat is headed by the taluk development officer (TDO), who has quite a few development departments like primary education, health, agriculture, veterinary under him. Most development programmes like Small Farmers Development Agency, Marginal Farmers and Agricultural Labourers Agency, IRDP, Tribal Sub-Plan are implemented through the TDO's office.

The taluk also has other government offices not part of the panchayati raj system. The revenue department is one of the oldest and well established departments headed by a *mamlatdar*. This is a very powerful position because it deals with land, land revenue and land records. In fact, the *mamlatdar* is the administrative arm of the state government at taluk level. He is the direct subordinate of the district collector at the district level and therefore enjoys all emergency powers of the district collector at taluk level.

The third tier of local government institutions is at the district level. The district has an elected council called zilla panchayat. This body is composed of directly elected members and also indirectly elected members representing taluk and village panchayats. Most programmes of rural development are administered by or through this body. The zilla panchayat has committees for health, education, etc. The head of the executive side is called District Development Officer (DDO), who belongs to the Indian Administrative Service (IAS). Under him are various departmental heads.

The other most important official at the district level is the collector who is also a district magistrate. Like the *mamlatdar* at taluk level, the collector, who belongs to the IAS, is traditionally the most important and powerful official of the state government at the district level which is the level from which all field operations begin. In spite of elected zilla panchayats and many other departments of the state government having their offices at the district level, the collector is the administrative head of the district and enjoys all emergency powers. He is in charge of land and revenue; civil supplies; district planning board of which he is the Chairman; and judicial functions.

Besides, most other government departments like forest, social welfare, public works, cooperatives and police have district level offices and officers. Some political parties also have district level units and offices. There are myriad of development programmes, schemes and projects being administered by different departments. Some programmes relevant for our purposes are: Tribal Sub-Plan in tribal districts implemented through relevant subject matter departments but expected to be monitored and coordinated by a separate Tribal Sub-Plan administrator; Integrated Rural Development Programme (IRDP); National Rural Development Programme (NRDP); Rural Landless Employment Guarantee Programme (RLEGP) implemented by District Rural Development Agency (DRDA); National Adult Education Programme (NAEP) being administered by a separate project office; Integrated Child Development Scheme (ICDS) and nutrition programme implemented by the health department; number of schemes and projects of agricultural development and other allied activities; *balwadis* (nursery schools) being financed by the Social Welfare

Department; Training of Rural Youth for Self-employment (TRYSEM) being implemented by DRDA. There are a bewildering variety of these schemes, projects and programmes and it is very difficult to obtain information on all programmes and agencies involved in them. The situation is quite confusing.

All these departments and agencies operate in the poor and backward areas of Sabarkantha and Panchmahals districts and in Dharampur taluk.

While it may be true that viewed from a gross level the input of money and other resources for development appear insufficient, looked specifically the amounts of money and the number of people allocated for development in these areas is amazingly large. We tried to find out how much money was spent in our two districts in a year, by all government agencies and other public institutions like cooperatives and banks, for rural development and the number of people employed in these organizations. We got hopelessly caught in planned and non-planned expenditure, state allocations and central allocations, state schemes and central schemes, normal programmes and vertical programmes and on and on. Nobody seems to have even an approximate idea of the amount of money spent in a district in a year by all departments and agencies and the number of people employed for rural development work.

In spite of all our efforts over a period of more than two months we could develop only a partial and incomplete picture which I suspect is not quite accurate even for departments for which we got information. Yet, even this partial and approximate picture is indeed revealing. Tables 3 and 4 present figures on expenditure and manpower of some of the rural development departments in Panchmahals and Sabarkantha districts.

Table 3 shows that in Panchmahals district seven government agencies involved in rural development spent more than Rs. 686 million in the year 1985–86 and in all 21,302 people were employed in these departments. If this amount is distributed equally among 1,909 villages of the district, each village would get more than Rs. 3,59,000 for the year 1985–86. If the employees from a peon to the highest officer were distributed equally among these 1,909 villages of Panchmahal each village would have 11.15 employees in residence. If the money spent in 1985–86 by only these seven agencies were distributed equally among all rural people of the district—men,

Table 3

Expenditure and Personnel for Rural Development in Some of the Departments in Panchmahals District (1985–86)

Sl. No.	Government Agencies	No. of employees	Expenditure in Rupees				No. of employees per village
			During 1985–86	Per village (1909* villages)	Per Household (300765** rural households)	Per Capita (Rural Population: 2321689)	
1.	Panchayat bodies in the district	14,757	43,49,51,142	2,27,842	1,446.1	187.3	7.73
2.	PWD roads and buildings division	101	1,91,55,000	10,034	63.6	8.2	0.05
3.	Forest Department:						
	a. Panchmahals Dist. Irrigation	72	54,79,930	2,871	18.2	2.3	0.03
	b. Dahod Division	158	93,00,000	4,872	30.9	4.0	0.08
	c. Godhra Division	188	92,93,340	4,868	30.9	4.0	0.09
	d. Godhra (Divisional Extension)	153	92,02,000	4,820	30.6	3.9	0.08
4.	Irrigation Department (Godhra)	219	1,65,33,000	8,661	54.9	7.1	0.11
5.	Tribal sub-plan (Dahod)	25	16,96,54,000	88,871	564.0	73.0	0.01
5.	Rural Development Agency	35	1,18,70,000	6,218	39.4	5.1	0.01
7.	I.C.D.S.	5,594	13,70,000	718	4.5	0.6	2.95
	Total	21,302	68,68,08,412	3,59,775	2,283.1	295.5	11.14

* According to 1981 census.

** This is actually a number of residential buildings according to 1971 census.

TABLE 4

Expenditure and Personnel for Rural Development in Some of the Departments in Sabarkantha District (1985–86)

Sl. No.	Particulars	No. of employees	Expenditure in Rupees				No. of employees per village
			During 1985–86	Per village (1,386 villages)	Per Household (3,36,060 rural households)	Per Capita (Rural Population: 13,40,000)	
1.	Panchayat bodies in the district	9,212	13,31,01,955	96,033	396.01	99.3	6.64
2.	Forest Department:						
	Office	259	32,54,836	2,348	10.7	2.4	0.18
	North Extension	124	71,75,000	5,177	21.6	5.3	0.09
	South Extension	124	72,75,000	5,249	21.6	5.4	0.08
3.	Rural Development Agency	44	95,36,000	6,880	28.4	7.1	0.03
4.	Irrigation (PWD)	951	8,06,85,000	58,214	240.1	60.2	0.68
5.	Roads and buildings (PWD)	200 (approx.)	10,00,00,000 (approx.)	72,150	297.8	74.6	0.14
6.	Tribal Sub-Plan	26	30,00,082	2,164	8.9	2.2	0.02
7.	I.C.D.S. – Regular	260	1,71,04,300	12,341	50.9	12.7	0.18
	– Irregular	4,260	—	—	—	—	3.10
	Total	15,460	36,11,32,173	2,60,557	1,075.7	269.2	11.14

women and children, rich and poor, tribal and non-tribal—each person would get Rs. 295 per year. Similarly in Sabarkantha for the same year each village would get more than Rs. 260,000 and 11.21 employees (Table 4).

It must be noted that the total amount of money for rural development poured into these districts would be far higher than what is shown here, because many other agencies and departments directly or indirectly involved in rural development are not included in these tables.

Context of the Mandals

All these mandals operate in predominantly backward areas. As mentioned earlier these villages are predominantly or fully tribal. Only two groups in Sabarkantha, Mota Kantharia and Poshina, are in bigger town-like villages with mixed population including a good sprinkling of higher and intermediate castes. Two cooperative societies of Thuris in Sabarkantha, where most members live in small towns, Gambhoi and Dhansura, doing bamboo work, have really no permanent residence in terms of village or town. They are nomadic tribes. The bamboo workers group in Gambhoi have their huts adjacent to the highway but they shift from time to time.

Gujarat has a relatively better infrastructure of facilities like roads, public transportation, electricity and markets; but the areas where these groups operate have few of these facilities. Electricity has not yet reached some groups in Sabarkantha and most groups in Panchmahals and Dharampur. The seven groups in Sabarkantha of the Isri-Kundol area (Mota Kantharia, Jalampur, Vanta, Chhitadara, Kagda Mahuda, Isri-Kundol and Isri-Kundol Mahila Mandal) have *kuchcha* rubble roads. (Villagers complained that they had to change their bicycle tyres and tubes every six months, and flat tyres was a thrice-a-week phenomenon). Public buses halt at these villages between one to three times a day and that too irregularly as now and then trips are cancelled because of breakdowns, paucity of buses or simply because drivers do not turn up.

All the groups, except those that are in Dharampur, operate in rain-scarcity areas and both Sabarkantha and Panchmahals are officially considered drought-prone areas. In the past, irrigation if at all possible, was based on private wells, before some groups undertook small irrigation activity. Agriculture is generally backward and production is low. Both Panchmahals and Sabarkantha where these groups work are predominantly one-crop areas, and therefore, incidence of seasonal migration is high though much higher and severer in Panchmahals. Panchmahals' tribals migrate to distant areas for periods of six to eight months. This has hampered the activities of the groups, as very few young men are left in the villages, membership becomes irregular, and sometimes recovery of loans is also delayed. In Dharampur, too, seasonal migration is very high and therefore groups are not able to undertake many activities in a concerted way. In Sabarkantha, in the area of the Isri-Kundol groups, incidence of seasonal migration is limited. While tribals do go out of their villages in search of labour it is generally to the surrounding areas and they return home in the evenings or visit their homes frequently. Both in Sabarkantha and Panchmahals as also in Dangs and Dharampur, penetration of developmental activities or public authorities has been limited, as compared to political penetration—electioneering, political linkages and political interaction. In Dharampur, Dangs and Panchmahals and to a lesser extent in the Isri-Kundol area of Sabarkantha, many positions in development agencies of the government remain vacant. Lower level field functionaries in the departments of health, education, agriculture, veterinary medicine etc., do not reside at their official headquarters. Incidence of absenteeism and locked offices is high. In fact, some mandals in Dharampur had to take recourse to agitation and direct action (like locking the school building) in order to get the primary schools to operate as teachers rarely attended their schools in these villages. They also had to agitate to ensure the presence of staff at the primary health centre. Even now, out of nearly forty staff members in the Pindwal primary health centre only three live in the headquarter village.

Even voluntary development agencies from outside have not touched these areas in any significant way. There has been more voluntary action in Dharampur in the last twenty years and more cooperative activity (if it can any more be called voluntary) in Dangs. There are some Ashramshalas* in the areas of Dangs, Sabarkantha and Panchmahals. There has been some Christian missionary activity and one often comes across tribals who proudly

---

* Ashramshalas are primary and secondary residential schools run by large voluntary agencies of the Gandhian type. They almost entirely depend on government grants.

introduce themselves as Christian tribals. Gamdi and its surrounding villages had seen considerable missionary activity in the past, particularly in the field of education; Gamdi village was reported to have nearly 85 per cent literacy. The missionary establishment at Lusadia nearer the groups of the Isri-Kundol area have been involved in educational and economic developmental activities somewhat similar to what these groups do. Similarly, in Dharampur too there is a Christian missionary establishment. Some Hindu sects have now started their establishments in Dharampur. I even came across a Jain establishment.

If one were to rank the various areas in which these groups work on the basis of the criteria of backwardness, suffering and oppression, Dharampur and Dangs—nearly hundred per cent tribal areas—would rank first, Panchmahals would rank next along with the tribal area of the Khedbrahma taluk of Sabarkantha district, and last would be the area of the seven groups adjoining Isri-Kundol in Meghraj and Bhiloda taluk of Sabarkantha District.

The people of Dharampur, Dangs and Khedbrahma taluk of Sabarkantha district have retained more of their tribal ways of life, than those of Meghraj and Bhiloda taluk of Sabarkantha. Fewer tribals in these areas are in government service, as compared to tribals of Meghraj and Bhiloda taluk of Sabarkantha. Incidence of drinking and illicit distillation is much higher in Dharampur, Dangs and Panchmahals, than in Sabarkantha. During our overnight stay in Gamdi and Nagvav in Panchmahals we met, saw or heard many people deeply intoxicated including two leaders of groups and several members. As against that we never came across a single incident of drunkenness during our much longer stay in Isri-Kundol in Meghraj taluk. The Poshina area of Khedbrahma taluk in Sabarkantha is indeed backward and poverty-stricken. Very little developmental activity is noticeable. Rival groups of tribals fight in the manner of battles invading each other's villages with bows and arrows. Murders are also not uncommon and the hold of traditional leaders and tribal customs is still strong. As the president of the Tembda Cooperative Society said, 'We are seventy years behind the tribals of Meghraj and Bhiloda taluk.'

A larger number of tribals, including group leaders, in Meghraj and Bhiloda taluk have government jobs than group members in Dharampur, Dangs and Panchmahals. Their exposure to things modern, urban and 'upper' is much more. As a British friend of mine who accompanied us during our visit to Isri-Kundol area ruefully remarked, 'They are hinduised.'

In the larger context two things may be noted here. First, corruption, oppression, exploitation, cheating and even physical suppression by the modern sector is much more than that by the traditional sector. The traditional landlords, money-lenders or the proverbial bania have increasingly given way to politicians and their brokers, bureaucrats and their collaborators, contractors in the fields of labour, forest and transportation, and cooperative societies and banks. Because these agencies are modern their effects are severer and recourse to relief more difficult. Moreover, some of these politicians and lower level bureaucrats who form clique for exploitation and oppression are tribals themselves.

Second, in spite of these generally debilitating conditions, the situation in Gujarat is much better than in many other states like Rajasthan, Madhya Pradesh, Uttar Pradesh, Bihar or Orissa. It is so possibly because Gujarat has a long tradition of Gandhian constructive and social work. Consequently, spread of educational activities has been much wider in backward areas of Gujarat than in similar areas in other states. It is not uncommon to find second and even third generation educated tribals in some of these areas, because of the widespread educational activities of Gandhian voluntary agencies since 1925. There is also, therefore, a general atmosphere of acceptance of tribal uplift. Big landlordism as found in the northern states is nearly absent here. And almost every tribal owns some land. Both in Panchmahals and Sabarkantha we did not come across a single case of a landlord owning even 100 acres of land. Landlords armed with guns and goons are not common in Gujarat. Though it is true that some groups had to put up a stiff fight against vested interests and that there were attempts to harass and intimidate them, such cases have been few and restrained. Such problems, it may again be noted, were faced more by groups in Dangs, Panchmahals and Khedbrahma taluk than by groups of the Isri-Kundol area. Politics and bureaucracy are as yet not very highly criminalized and brutalized in Gujarat.*

* One hears that such criminalization is much more in Saurashtra region of Gujarat which is quite feudal and where similar group activities have not taken place. One also comes across a feeling becoming increasingly widespread, that brutalization of politics and bureaucracy is increasing in Gujarat and that it would soon catch up with the others.

In the face of opposition, as we shall see, unscrupulous elements in politics, bureaucracy or business and agriculture usually, though not always, tend to retreat rather than react more violently. The environment in Gujarat is therefore more viable for such group activities.

3

Formation and Organization

Genesis

Some of the groups have started their activities very recently, while some had started in a small way much earlier than 1979. The period covered here is from 1979 to 1984.

When in 1979 OXFAM decided to shift its emphasis from larger and established voluntary agencies to small groups and support them with small amounts of funds, a few of these groups were already in existence and trying to do some economic and other developmental activities. Thus the Isri-Kundol,[1] Vantda Milk Cooperative, Navavenpur, Chunakhan, Gambhoi groups in Sabarkantha and Zalod, Satkunda Cooperative and Sagtala Co-operative were formed before 1979.

A sizable number of groups, nine out of thirty-eight were formed before OXFAM's involvement with small groups started. Twenty-four of the thirty-eight groups are between two to four years old. It may seem that the activity of forming such groups has decreased in the last two years as only three of these groups are less than two years old. In fact, quite a few groups have been formed in the last two to three years but are not included here as they have not received OXFAM support and, therefore, were not included in the list provided to us.

Once some of these groups received financial support from OXFAM they in turn talked to their friends, relatives and acquaintances in the surrounding villages about forming similar groups. They provided information about OXFAM, procedures for forming and registering the groups and their organization. Majority of the groups,

[1] For the sake of convenience various groups are referred to here by names of their villages rather than their full formal names which are sometimes long and cumbersome.

nearly twenty-six of the thirty-eight that we had opportunity to study, were formed by the encouragement of other groups.

The Process of Initial Formation

In all groups barring the cooperative societies, generally two or three younger people of the village in the twenty-five to forty-five age group would take the initiative. In most cases these were tribal youth, with at least primary education, often working in some government or semi-government organizations like cooperative societies. They would discuss with other young people like themselves the idea of forming an organization. Once sufficient interest or curiosity was generated among eight or ten people, a general meeting of the villagers was called by them. Since it was difficult to generate sufficient interest among the people for attending the meeting, young people who had taken the initiative would broach the subject and try to garner general support during a gathering of villagers, be it for some religious festival, *bhajan*[2] singing sessions or even during a marriage.

But before calling a general meeting considerable discussion and consultation would take place among the few who had taken the initiative. Almost always older people, the traditional leaders of the tribe or the village, were avoided during these initial discussions: 'They are *khokhas* (empty boxes); they have "old thoughts" and would dampen our enthusiasm.' There was also an underlying apprehension that since such activities would threaten their hold, either they would not support it or would try to control it. It may be noted here that barring five cooperative societies and a women's group, twenty-nine of the remaining thirty-two groups have the word 'youth' as part of their officially registered names.

The initial response of the village people in general was always lukewarm. The main reasons were: (a) general inertia and indifference towards secular group activities; (b) deep pessimism—'nothing ever really happens'; (c) lurking suspicion that these things are generally political; and (d) strong and widespread distrust of fellow-villagers in matters of money. In many villages, particularly in Panchmahals, incidents were narrated to us where

[2] All villages have *bhajan mandalis*, where on religious occasions or some fixed days of a month (e.g., full moon day or the eleventh day) people of the village get together to sing devotional songs.

people were cheated by some who collected money for forming a cooperative, or for getting subsidies and loans from the government for bullocks or wells, and then vanished.

The initiators, therefore, had often to put in money from their own pockets for the initial expenses of registration fees, travel to the Commissioner's office, buying stationery, postage etc. In a few cases, a small group of people was put together for official registration purposes and enrolling ordinary members was done later on.

Organization

As mentioned earlier all groups barring the cooperative societies are registered as public trusts or as societies with the Charity Commissioner. They all have a constitution. Most mandals have identical constitutions as they were copied from some other mandal. Mandals have various types of membership such as ordinary, life and patrons. In reality, however, only one type of membership exists: the ordinary membership. All the mandals have executive committees comprising nine to eleven members, with positions of president, vice-president, secretary and treasurer.

Some mandals also have one or two joint secretaries. In some cases the executive committee is supposed to meet once a month, while in most groups it is once in three months. The general meeting of ordinary members is once a year and in some cases twice a year.

Most mandals, twenty-four out of the thirty-eight, were found to be holding executive committee meetings pretty regularly. Though very few met formally once a month throughout the year, the executive committee members, particularly the office bearers would meet very frequently, informally, to discuss mandal matters.

The general body meetings, however, are not very regular. In case of nearly eight groups the general body, it seemed, had not met for more than a year. Some groups, however, are very regular. All Dharampur groups are involved in the activity of loaning food grains, called *khavti*. They hold their general meetings twice a year while giving and recovering food grain loans. Attendance at these meetings is high and regular. Poshina group holds four general meetings in a year and have adopted the rule of expelling a member who remains absent for more than three meetings consecutively. For groups who had maintained records of proceedings, the maximum attendance was rarely found to be more than 60 per cent barring exceptions like Poshina or Dharampur. It may be mentioned that some groups have no idea that they should maintain the *tharav* book (record of resolutions). Some, in their record of proceedings had not recorded the attendance with signatures of those who attended but had only taken down the decisions reached. Quite often meetings were not handled in a formal and structured way. During the general body meetings many villagers who are not members participate and ask questions. Sometimes a gathering of villagers for a religious or social occasion is utilized to discuss the mandal's activities. In our assessment, nearly five of the six groups in the two districts which have not been able to become very active and have stagnated, and nearly six groups which are progressively becoming inactive and are in danger of disintegration, are irregular in holding meetings and indifferent to group participation and group decision-making.

OXFAM Support

I have given in Appendix 2 a separate and more detailed account of OXFAM's role and involvement in the activities of small action groups but here I am very briefly describing OXFAM's financial support to these groups.

OXFAM began to look for appropriate opportunities to support small groups of weaker sections in 1979. Since then it has been giving small sums of money ranging from Rs. 10,000 to Rs. 70,000 per group. The funds are given as loans or grants.

These funds are mainly given for economic activities. In a few cases OXFAM has given smaller amounts of Rs. 1,000 to Rs. 3,000 as administrative grants to what are called core groups for travelling, stationery and similar administrative expenses. To some groups like Isri-Kundol, Zalod or Pindval, OXFAM has given single-purpose or special specific grants for holding training camps or *shibirs*.

Core Groups

Some of the groups have been identified and referred to as core groups by OXFAM.[3] They are so called because they propagate

---

[3] Neither the groups nor any of their leaders are formally recognized or designated as core.

the idea of group activities in the surrounding villages where there were no groups. They identify young men who have potentiality and who have shown some interest, and then encourage them to form groups. There are seven such groups: Kundawada, Jamran, Vangad, Gamdi and Abhlod in Panchmahals district and Sabar Yuva Vikas Mandal and Isri-Kundol groups in Sabarkantha district. Besides, some groups which are not identified as core groups also play the role of informing other villages and encouraging them to form group. Thus, Poshina, one of the best and most active groups in Sabarkantha, came to know about OXFAM through a neighbouring group of the same taluk.

Core groups, besides encouraging others to start developmental activities, help them with advice and information about OXFAM, registration procedures, formation of executive committees, membership, maintaining of accounts, and procedures for advancing loans and their recovery.

Once the groups are formed core groups seem to lose interest in their activities or problems. Their help is generally confined to initial formation, framing the constitution and procedures, registration and accounts. The Panchmahals core groups are somewhat more active than the two core groups of Sabarkantha. Even in Panchmahals by 1983, the core groups, except the one in Gamdi, seemed to have become passive in their mobilization work. The Gamdi group has been very active and instrumental in getting many groups formed. Some of these groups have been functioning for nearly two years now but have not received OXFAM funds. The Gamdi group also helps other groups in identifying activities to undertake and other sources of funding.

In Sabarkantha both the core groups seem to have become passive. During our visit the president of the Isri-Kundol group accompanied us to some groups which he had helped form. But it was clear that he had subsequently lost touch with them; he did not know who the office bearers were and had very little information on how these groups functioned.

In all core groups, however, it is generally one person who performs the function of helping other groups; the group as a whole is not involved.

Some core groups have stagnated or declined. The Jamran group is in the process of disintegration. Vangad seems to be stagnating. Even Kundawada has not remained as active as it was initially. In Isri-Kundol, while the executive members are still active, it is not clear whether they still retain interest in the basic idea of the group. They seem to have taken up other activities while the group itself seems to be turning somewhat passive.

The idea of core groups, however, is an excellent one and has generally worked very well. The formation of new groups would not have taken place so quickly and in such numbers, without the help of such groups. The idea of small action groups of weaker sections has taken root more quickly through the efforts of the core groups. The idea of the 'independence' of the functioning of small group is carried and maintained much better when they are formed with the help of similar groups from their own area, rather than with the help of well established agencies from outside. This way it is clear to the newly-formed groups that they must learn to manage their own affairs because the core group is also small and surviving on meagre resources. The core group members are not 'experts' and therefore the new groups have to start thinking about how to go about doing things. Thus, they begin to assume responsibility and learn to cope right from the start. The newly-formed groups are not as overwhelmed and dependent as they would be if they had the sponsorship and auspices of well established, resourceful agencies of 'professionalized' developers.

There is, however, a need to reassess the role of core groups in the two districts where a number of small groups are already working. In Panchmahals, for instance, this role can be taken up by the district level body of the union of mandals in Panchmahals. In Sabarkantha, the formation of new groups seems to have slowed down and the district level union of mandals has not as yet taken off. There may be a need to identify one or two more groups as core groups, or to encourage and reactivate Isri-Kundol. In these two districts, the core groups can also help the already functioning groups to get together in small numbers, say four to six groups from adjoining villages. This may also provide an opportunity for ordinary members, other than office bearers and executive committee members, to get together; which is very necessary. This is a point I propose to discuss in some detail later on. The groups have been doing some informal self-assessment, but there is also a need for more systematic self-assessment. There are, for instance, a number of groups which are facing problems of recovery of loans, of dwindling or increasing membership, of stagnation and so on.

While the leaders are aware of this, they often do nothing about it. A more explicit collective reassessment along with others, but in small numbers only, would motivate them to do something. Here the core groups can play a catalytic role of gentle prodding.

Some groups are totally isolated. The two cooperative societies of bamboo workers and the Navavenpur groups of Sabarkantha have very little information about, or interaction with, any other group in Sabarkantha. The cooperative societies of bamboo workers and the milk cooperative society at Vantda did not know about the core groups nor much about the two core persons. Core groups can take on the role of initiating interaction between groups. Statewide *shibirs* attended by 100 or more participants cannot perform this function effectively.

4

Members and Leaders

Size

As mentioned earlier the constitution of the groups provide for various types of membership. However, in actuality only one type, yearly, ordinary membership, exists.

Table 5 provides data about the membership of various mandals. Chitadara group has the lowest membership of 21, while Abhlod has the highest membership of 235. Most groups, twenty-five of the thirty-eight, have membership ranging from twenty-five to 100. Ten groups have membership between 100 and 200, three groups have membership above 200. This gives an idea of how small these groups are.

TABLE 5
Size of Groups by Membership

District/ Taluk	Membership				
	25 or less	*26 to 50*	*51 to 100*	*101 to 200*	*201 to 300*
Sabarkantha	1	7	3	4	—
Panchmahals	—	3	1	5	2
Dharampur	—	2	8	1	1
Total	1	12	12	10	3

It is also noteworthy that Sabarkantha district does not have any high membership groups, while it has the only group with a membership of less than 25, the Chitadara mandal. Three of the four mandals in this district with a membership of more than 100 are cooperatives where organizational matters like membership, record maintenance, dues collection have been relatively more regular as they are inspected and audited by the cooperatives department regularly.

In as many as twenty-five out of thirty-eight groups the membership has remained stagnant, and in the case of the Zalod group of Panchmahals, one of the oldest and a self-mobilized group, membership has declined.

However, the data presented in Table 5 does not provide adequate understanding about the membership. For instance, some groups have not increased their membership even when more villagers wished to join as they had limited funds for advancing loans. Chunakhan in Sabarkantha admitted five more Thakarda members only last year, after considerable hesitation. Jalampur, Poshina and Mithibor, for instance, have received feelers from villagers for new membership, but the leaders were still debating whether new members should be taken or not because of the resource constraint.

Very few groups maintain a regular yearly register of members. In fact, some groups consider loanees too as their members. In most cases membership fees have been collected only once and membership fees are not received regularly. Even after two to three years intensive activities, the leaders have found that members do not come on their own to pay their membership dues. For instance, Gamdi and Abhold of Panchmahals have been very active mandals. Their activities have benefited the whole village as also other villages covered by the mandal. And yet they have not been able to increase their membership in the third and fourth years. These mandals have been instrumental in starting several organizations as spin-off, but many villagers who are involved in the new organizations and have benefited by them are not members of the mandal. In Gamdi, not only have no new members been enrolled in the last two years, only two members had paid their membership fees for 1984, although fees were overdue for more than one year. On the other hand, Poshina has been getting its membership fees regularly though its membership has increased to fifty from an initial twenty-one, and it also has a rule that members must attend three meetings in a year. In fact, it has increased its membership fees from Rs. 11 to Rs. 21.

Caste

Out of the thirty-eight groups under study, five groups in Sabarkantha, four groups in Panchmahals, the Mithibor group of

Chhotaudaipur taluk and all twelve groups of Dharampur taluk have exclusive tribal membership. Six groups are predominantly adivasi while three of the groups in Sabarkantha are predominantly or exclusively non-adivasi. Two of these are of Thuris or bamboo-workers, and one, a milk co-operative society, is of Thakardas.

The predominantly adivasi groups have a few members from Thakarda[1] or Harijan castes in Sabarkantha, and Harijan or Koli-Bariyas[1] in Panchmahals. For instance, Chunakhan in Sabarkantha has only recently taken five Thakarda members in what its president called 'a test case.' Navavenpur has members from Harijan, Thakarda and Prajapati or potters castes.

Sometimes, in predominantly adivasi groups the office bearers are non-adivasi. In Kundawada the secretary is a Rajput and the president a Koli-Bariya. Poshina, which is a backward adivasi area has a Muslim president, adivasi vice-president and secretary from a scheduled caste. But in spite of the presence of non-adivasi members the identity of these groups is strongly adivasi. Their names also bear the word adivasi. The groups with non-adivasi office bearers tend to take up activities that also directly help non-adivasi backward groups in their area. Lavaria, for instance, pays as much attention towards benefit of Koli-Bariyas as to the adivasis. And Poshina had taken up the issue of minimum wages which is largely related to scheduled caste labourers.

In Sabarkantha, the Thakardas are socially and economically more backward than the adivasis. The various adivasi office bearers that we talked to, frankly admitted that the adivasis are more advanced and dominant as compared to Thakardas in Meghraj and Bhiloda taluks. The few Thakardas whom we could meet also admitted that they are backward and more heavily in debt as compared to the adivasis. Moreover, they are in debt more to private money-lenders, traders and landlords than adivasis whose debts are now largely to institutions like banks, cooperative societies or the government. There is also a higher incidence among the Thakardas of Sabarkantha of putting their younger children as *khedu*[2] on the farms of bigger landholders against the debt that

[1] Both these are backward groups included in the Baxi Panch as socially and economically backward (SEBC).

[2] *Khedu* is a system in which a young boy works on an yearly basis on the farm of a bigger landholder. The official rate is Rs. 3,600 but most get under Rs. 3,000 a year and sometimes as low as Rs. 1,500. *Khedu* system seems to be a milder version

they have incurred. Because of a low level of education they rarely get into government jobs. On the other hand many adivasis from the villages of the Isri-Kundol area are in government jobs. In Isri-Kundol village alone, according to the estimate of its president, as many as twenty-five families had atleast one member in government service.

It seems that in the adivasi-Thakardas relationship in these villages, the adivasis tend to dominate. Reportedly, adivasis have begun to extend personal loans to Thakardas against land as collateral. In Isri-Kundol village itself, at least three cases of adivasis, who are active leaders of the mandal, buying up land of the Thakardas were reported to us.

Mandal leaders find it difficult to advance loans to them because they are doubtful about recovery. The few Thakardas that we met and talked to admitted as much.

Since the mandals have become active in these villages it is very likely that any future inputs of any kind from outside, as also interaction with the outside world will be through and under the influence of these mandals. In that case the Thakardas or the scheduled castes will be further pushed to the periphery.

A much more concerted effort to mobilize and organize these castes is required. Such an effort cannot be confined to economic activities alone, and will require equal emphasis on educational awareness and social action activities. It will have to be specifically and perhaps exclusively directed towards the marginal groups in these villages. These efforts will have to be of a viable size and intensity right from the beginning. Half-hearted and diffident inputs will not yield results.

The modalities of such efforts may vary depending on the local situation:

(a) In cases where such peripheral groups are in sizable numbers, as in Isri-Kundol where nearly fifty of the 110 households and twenty-seven of the sixty-five members of the mandal are Thakardas, efforts could be made through the existing mandal. The mandal can develop a special fund exclusively for these groups, it can be helped to mount membership drives, information and awareness

---

of bonded labour and quite often this is towards the payment of debts, incurred by the father, uncle or elder brother.

camps etc. Poshina in Sabarkantha has office bearers from different castes, and looking at the approach and orientation of mandal leaders Poshina seems to be a promising group for these kind of activities. The president of Chunakhan mandal showed a willingness during our discussions to earmark funds exclusively for Thakardas if such a fund was made available to the mandal. He, however, said that the Thakardas prefer to identify with the higher caste of Rajputs and it was doubtful whether they would like to get involved with adivasis. He also suggested that an effective strategy for bringing about 'reform' and change among Thakardas would be to work through a religious leader and generate a religion-based reform movement.

(*b*) Another alternative could be to start separate and independent activities exclusively for these groups which would cover several villages. Two or three groups can be established at nodal points in the district. The president of the Isri-Kundol mandal helped to start an Ashramshala for Thakardas. The possibility of building up other activities around the Ashramshala can be explored. The Vantda Milk-Cooperative is exclusively manned and managed by Thakardas, and in its limited activity it is well managed. This group has greater potentiality and some activities can be generated around this group.

Whatever the modalities, greater effort is needed for such castes who are very backward, who have as yet not been touched by government or voluntary agencies' programmes, and who may be in danger of being further pushed to the periphery because of the activities of some of these mandals.

Background of the Leaders

As mentioned earlier, mandals have a number of office bearers. All mandals have a president, vice-president and secretary. Some mandals also have a joint-secretary and/or treasurer. Most of these office bearers are quite young. The oldest president is fifty-six years old from Chunakhan and the youngest is twenty-one years old from Poshina. Poshina also has the youngest secretary who is twenty. Of the thirty-eight groups on which we have gathered data, the average age of various positions is: 33.4 years for the president, 33.3 years for the vice-president and secretary, 33.5

years for the joint secretary/treasurer, and 33.4 years for all office bearers considered together.

All office bearers except two belong to backward castes, tribes, scheduled castes, Koli Bariyas and Thakardas. The Khundawada group in Panchmahals has a Rajput secretary and the Poshina group has a Muslim president.

Information on educational levels is given in Table 6. There are six groups where the majority of executive members have education up to high school level or above. In ten groups, majority of the members have education up to primary level or even less. Gambhoi Bamboo Workers' Cooperative, for instance, has mostly illiterate leaders and members. Even the president can barely sign his name.

TABLE 6
Educational Level of Executive Committee Members

District/Taluk	Groups where majority of Executive Committee members have education up to primary level or less	Groups where 3 to 4 members have education up to high school level	Groups where majority of executive members have education up to high school level or above	Not ascertained
Sabarkantha	5	4	4	2
Panchmahals	5	2	2	2
Dharampur	12	—	—	—
Total	22	6	6	4

In most mandals, even where office bearers and a majority of the members had education up to high school level or above, they had never handled or managed as large a sum of money as Rs. 40,000. Leaders of mandals in Dharampur and Mithibor never had any dealings with a bank before and had not even seen a bank passbook or a cheque. For instance, the OXFAM Field Officer had promised to send money to the Mithibor group. However, when a cheque arrived members felt cheated by the outsider who had made them a false promise, raised their hopes and only sent them a piece of paper. Some groups like Gambhoi and Vantda Vatrak Cooperatives had to hire an outsider as a secretary. The

Mithibor president had to request a friend from Jamran group to act as a secretary while the Navavenpur president took the help of his wife for all correspondence.

It may be noted that a larger number of groups in Sabarkantha have members who are more educated than the Panchmahals groups. In Dharampur ten out of twelve presidents, eleven out of twelve vice-presidents and eight out of twelve secretaries have education only up to the 7th grade (Table 7).

TABLE 7
Educational Level of Office Bearers

Position	From 1st to 7th grade	From 8th to 10th grade	High School and above	Not ascertained
Sabarkantha District				
President	6	2	6	1
Vice-President	6	3	3	3
Secretary	—	6	7	2
Panchmahals District				
President	4	4	4	—
Vice-President	2	3	2	4
Secretary	3	4	2	2
Dharampur Taluk				
President	10	2	0	—
Vice-President	11	0	1	—
Secretary	8	4	0	—

Table 8 presents data on the occupation of the office bearers. Nearly ten of the thirty-five groups for which we could gather information, have at least two out of three or four office holders who have jobs in government or semi-government bodies like cooperative societies, state transport corporation, and primary schools. Many of them are employed as primary school teachers, but a few also work in other government departments: the Abhlod president is with the telephones department and the Gamdi president is in the health department.

All office holders have some land and therefore are also involved in agriculture. It is very difficult to ascertain exact landholdings. Landholdings may be individual, jointly with the family, seasonal or yearly as with the submerged lands of the reservoir in Sabarkantha's Isri-Kundol area, or mortgaged land against

TABLE 8
Occupation of the Office Bearers

District/ Taluk	Groups where all the 3 or 3 out of 4 office holders are in service	Groups where 2 out of 3 or 4 office bearers are in service	Groups where only one office bearer is in service	Groups where not a single office bearer is in service	Not ascertained
Sabarkantha	2	4	2	5	2
Panchmahals	2	2	3	3	1
Dharampur	—	—	6	6	—
Total	4	6	11	14	3

personal loans. Some cultivate the land of others. Some leaders of Sabarkantha groups have landholdings in Sabarkantha as well as in Rajasthan.

Though, most groups and their leaders have provided information on landholdings to OXFAM, the information does not always reveal correct total landholing and especially the income out of the various types of landholdings. However, the general pattern that we could ascertain was that many (though not all) leaders in the Isri-Kundol area groups own or cultivate between seven to twenty acres of land. Some of them have recently bought land as a result of improved economic conditions, resulting from several years of service and supplementary economic activities. But from what we could ascertain, leaders of the groups in Khedbrahma taluk, and of all but one group in Panchmahals own less than five acres of land. In Dharampur many leaders as also members have a family holding of between eight to twenty acres. However, this land is not fertile as the region is hilly. Moreover, most cannot afford inputs like improved seeds or fertilizers. They grow only one crop, and often as much as half the land remains uncultivated. Though on paper they own sizable land because of family ownership, each person or his individual family does not own more than three to six acres. The leaders of the Dharampur groups are very poor.

Leaders who hold jobs have a regular income and therefore their involvement in the mandal's activities do not create problems of economic insecurity for them. They are, if necessary, able to spend some money for travel, stationery etc., from their own pockets for the mandal's activities. They travel to taluk and district headquarters oftener and also combine the mandal's work with their personal and office work. Since they are educated and interact with the outer world more often (towns, government offices, urbanized educated people) they have developed skills and confidence in interacting with the government officers for the mandal's or community's work, and are not easily misled, overawed or intimidated. They can bring useful information to the mandal members and the community about the government's development programmes and rules, regulations and procedures.

Their limitation is that they have to often stay outside the village and cannot find enough time to devote to the mandal's activities, particularly mobilizational and participative activities. They also find it difficult to participate when the group or the community has to undertake direct confrontational or agitational steps against local bureaucracy or politics. This, however, also depends on the orientation and commitment of the educated and employed leaders. For instance, generally leaders of the groups in Bhiloda and Meghraj taluks in Sabarkantha (except Jalampur), tend to concentrate more on economic and developmental activities than mobilizational, social action and struggle-oriented activities. The leaders of both Gamdi and Abhlod initially devoted a lot of time and attention to their groups and generated many activities which were mobilizational and participative. They organized and participated in agitations in their communities. But as they started new organizations for developmental activities they become more and more involved in running and managing these and in the compromises and manipulatious involved in the running of such organizations.

Since the more educated leaders employed in government or other public organizations tend to be 'development-oriented' rather than 'movement-oriented' they make efforts to generate more institutionalized developmental activities. As we shall discuss later on in the section on spin-off activities they are eager to start other institutions like irrigation, dairy or poultry cooperatives and boarding homes for students. This gives them greater resources, more power and influence. But they also get involved in managing these and making all the compromises, manipulations and manoeuvring that generally go with it. In the process the activities of the mandal get undermined.

These educated, job-holding leaders while performing institutionalized activities develop styles, orientations and motivations quite similar to those of political leaders and representatives of the weaker sections who occupy positions in parties, public and government institutions.

Those leaders who are not employed regularly and are not very educated are able to give more time and intensive involvement. They are usually more participative in their approach and the involvement of other members in activities of their groups is higher. But their limitation is that they have inadequate information about government programmes, rules and laws. They have to struggle more to interact and 'reach' the taluk and district level government bodies. Moreover, their major problem is their own economic insecurity. Jamran and Chakalia groups in Panchmahals, Mithibor in Chhote Udaipur taluk, Lambadia and Poshina in Sabarkantha and most groups in Dharampur have leaders who are quite poor. They have very little land and whatever little supplementary economic activities they had, have suffered because of their involvement with mandals. As per our information, two leaders had approached OXFAM with the request for a small monthly remuneration.

The personal economic problem of leaders who do not hold regular jobs, have very little land and are themselves poor, is real and severe. However, if these leaders are paid from the group funds they will tend to loose their credibility with other members, and a paid position would almost inevitably generate jealousy and a power struggle within the group.

In such cases, there are two possibilities that can be explored. One is to identify such active individual leaders and help them start an income-generating project like a flour-mill, a shop or some other activity. This may not be done through the group or a funding agency like OXFAM. Possibilities may be explored to get them some help from existing government programmes like IRDP, TRYSEM, and Tribal Development Plans. Alternatively, assistance can be sought from some institution or an individual or a group of individuals.

The other alternative is to give them monetary remuneration channeled through an agency other than their group. This remuneration will not go with their position in the mandal but be given to them in their personal capacity. The sum will be small, highly discretionary, and payable for a short term only; but renewable after every six months or so. Its implications and effects can be assessed before every renewal. Either alternative would require a very careful and thorough assessment of each situation.

Relationship between Leaders and Members

The groups face opposition from established community leaders and also outsiders like government officials, established voluntary agencies and politicians. These are discussed in Chapters 5 and 6. But the mandals sometimes also suffer from internal dissension and conflicts.

In a majority of the groups the leadership has remained unchanged. Wherever there have been changes it is because of suspicion of misappropriation or malpractice. There have also been a few cases of tension between leaders and members, or between an office holder and the rest of the executive members. In most such cases, the individual concerned has been removed. Only in one case, some of the office holders and executive committee members left the mandal when they found that the president was not taking them into his confidence and when they suspected him of misappropriation of funds. In Kundawada in Panchmahals, the secretary had to resign because he did not involve other members of the executive committee in decision-making. Lambadia group in Khedbrahmma taluk had several changes of office holders. In some groups there have been continuous quarrels and tension among the executive committee members about misappropriation of funds and favouritism in advancing loans from the OXFAM fund. In Gamdi, an executive committee member was removed when he was found to have used another person as a front for getting a loan for a bullock in contravention of the criteria laid down by the mandal.

During our field trips we could identify six groups out of the thirty-eight in addition to a women's group in Panchmahals where there was a strong suspicion of the leaders misappropriating mandal funds for personal use.

Conflicts and tensions among office bearers, or between office bearers and members, usually arise in connection with economic activities and management of funds. Internal tensions and conflicts have harmed the groups more than the harm done by community leaders or outside vested interests. In such cases the mandal either stopped some of its activities and became stagnant or a process of decline and disintegration set in. Groups like Lambadia and Chhitadara have become stagnant because of alleged misappropriation of money by its office bearers. Zalod and Sanjoi (women's) groups have almost disintegrated. Jamran had almost met a similar fate but now seems to be on the path to recovery because differences have been patched up. Gundia, one of the early starters in Dharampur, has stopped all its activities. Generally the groups have not been very successful in managing internal conflicts well. The most common reaction is one of panic and of stopping all activities. The leaders stop calling meetings, try to remain away from the village, make themselves unavailable or avoid meeting members or outsiders regarding any group-related work.

It is here that a careful and restrained but effective outside intervention may be necessary.

In Sabarkantha, we could identify eight out of fifteen groups where most executive committee members take a keen interest in the group's activities and are highly involved in issues concerning the groups and the communities. In Panchmahals we found that there are six groups out of ten where all or most executive committee members are very active. In Mithibor, one of the most backward villages, the involvement of the members, both ordinary and executive, is generally high. In Dharampur, nine out of the twelve groups seem to have a high involvement on the part of executive committee members. The Gamdi mandal in Panchmahals had informally distributed different activities to different people on the basis of their special ability or some special facility they had. A lawyer member helps them in taking up legal matters, petitions etc. Those working in government offices and travel frequently take up work pending with government offices, and also try to push papers and files using their friends and acquaintances in government offices. Its president, Bhalabhai, who is well-versed in carrying out village surveys because of his job, designed a comprehensive survey for the village soon after the group was formed, to decide their action plan. The joint secretary of the mandal is a teacher and president of the taluk teachers' association. He takes up many educational matters such as regularity of teachers in schools of villages under the Gamdi mandal. The vice-president of the group, who belongs to Sanjoli village, is very active in mobilizing and organizing the people. Since he owns a motor-cycle, he can quickly cover the surrounding villages and goes from place to place mobilizing and organizing people for election, agitation or some movement for which the group needs mass support.

One general pattern, with some exceptions like Gamdi and Abhlod, is that those mandals where leaders are not very educated and not in government service are generally more participative and have greater involvement of executive members as well as ordinary members.

But by and large, among ordinary members, there is as yet no deep sense of involvement or belonging. It is true, as mentioned earlier, that those groups which take on larger social action activities, struggle and confrontation, satyagraha and agitation, are able to involve more members and non-members. But even this involvement is often sporadic.

There are a few groups which have been involving members in decision making, particularly in economic activities. But even this has generally not helped in creating a sense of belonging or a sense of 'owning' the group.

By and large the leaders of these groups do not know ways and means of involving and arousing the commitment of ordinary members.

Leaders of the older groups need to move in this direction with greater zeal and determination because they are in greater danger of stagnation and disintegration.

There are several ways of doing this:

1. Group leaders can call more frequent meetings of community members.
2. They can make a more systematic and formal assessment of their relationship with the members. This will enable them to pinpoint their weaknesses.
3. They may give specific responsibilities to ordinary members. These may be for short-term activities. For instance, some ordinary members can be given the responsibility of collecting membership fees and helping in the membership drive along with the leaders.
4. They can try to involve ordinary members in their interaction with outsiders, particularly in their interaction with the government administration.

5. It would also be very helpful if ordinary members of one group visit another group periodically and spend about half a day with them.
6. Special training camps, similar to the *shibirs*, can be organized for ordinary members.
7. Groups can adopt, wherever feasible, norms for changing at least one-third of the executive members every two or three years.

Types, Orientations and Capabilities of Leaders

It is very difficult to classify leadership. Different situations have thrown up different kinds of leaders. Their capabilities and orientations, ideologies and motivations differ. Nearly all have acquired experience in mobilization, organization and management through the mandals.

We have already mentioned that some leaders have tried to misappropriate mandal funds. Such cases are not many. However, in all such cases the leaders are generally educated up to high school level, well exposed to modern things, having some experience of working in Panchayats, government or cooperative societies. Generally, the more backward the groups the more honest they are.

On the other hand there are quite a few leaders who have a high degree of commitment. The president of the Poshina group, a Muslim and belonging to the more dominant and well-to-do community in the area, has identified himself completely with the adivasis and scheduled castes, and his group is one of the most participative and strong.

The president of Zalod group has demonstrated interest and skills in mobilizing people, though his own group is neglected. He was one of the few active leaders who organized a massive rally at Zalod against the Forest Bill. The president of the Gamdi mandal has shown amazing competence in mobilization and organization. His understanding of larger issues is also very high. The presidents of Lavaria, Mithibor and Poshina have struggled and fought against injustice and malpractices of the local bureaucracy despite harassment and at the cost of personal safety.

Many of these leaders have strong potentialities to extend themselves beyond their groups and to contribute in generating more interaction between groups, in networking and mobilization activities and to work as resource persons for other groups. In our view, with greater experience and exposure to such activities at other places they can contribute considerably to the phenomenon of 'small action groups of weaker sections' in Gujarat.

Tables 6, 7 and 8 which gave the educational and occupational background of leaders show that while leaders of quite a few groups are educationally backward and economically poor, several groups have educated leaders employed permanently and getting a steady income who can by no means be considered very poor. This raises the question as to what extent these groups can be considered as groups of poor when their leaders, though belonging to tribes and backward castes, are not really very poor?

Firstly, even when these leaders are not very poor they are not among the strong and rich families of the village. That is, none of these leaders come from families traditionally occupying an elite position in the village. Neither they nor their parents were landlords, members of political parties occupying positions in panchayat institutions, cooperatives or other public organizations. Some of the leaders have acquired these positions after having become mandal leaders and because of their work in the mandals. Secondly, while it may be ideal to have the 'last' man as the leader of his own people, in reality it is very difficult to find such men who are willing to and capable of talking on leadership roles.

Mistry, the OXFAM field officer, commenting on this aspect of mandal leadership wrote,

The ideal is that leadership is vested in the last man of the village and yet after becoming the leader he should still remain the last man of the village. Here I see contradictions. First of all it is very difficult to find the last man who has the capability to become a leader straightaway. Secondly, even if we found one such he would be so poor that he would hardly have any time to run the affairs of the mandal as he himself would be endlessly struggling to earn his livelihood. He would have the limitations, of time, very little money and the inability to cope with the hostility of vested interests from his village or outside.

Finally, the moment he became a leader he would change his life style and behaviour and acquire a certain sophistication which would distance him from the people at the bottom from whom he originally came. This change would be inevitable because of his interaction with local politicians, bureaucrats and other local elites on mandal work. In order to successfully interact with them his way of dressing, mannerisms, way of talking and communication would all change. All this would soon set him apart from the last man.

Mithibor Vibhag Adivasi Yuvak Mandal is a very good example of this. Bhaljibhai, its president, came from the very last man of the village. He soon established himself as a leader. But his work brought him into contact with district-level politicians and bureaucrats, traders and landlords and outside activists. The influence and power he acquired and the occasions he had to interact and get involved with the outside world automatically changed his language, manner of speech, behaviour and life style.[3]

The situation regarding regular changes in the mandal leadership is somewhat similar. Those who look at such grass-roots efforts romantically expect internal democracy and active participation of the people leading to regular changes in leadership. In reality it is difficult to find a different team of eight or ten young men from the weaker sections, willing and capable, springing up at regular intervals of every two to three years, to take up leadership of the mandals.

What has motivated these relatively young men who do get involved in the mandals? From my long conversations with them I could observe a mixed set of motivations.

1. Some of these young men had traumatic experiences in their early youth of being insulted, humiliated or rejected because of their social position. Some developed the idealism during their school days.
2. Some being smart men with spark and not having found any opportunity through parties, elections and other political institutions saw in the mandals an opportunity to do something and scope for self-actualization.
3. Others saw in mandals the opportunity to raise their own status and influence in the community and also to fulfil their political ambitions.

[3] Quoted with language editing from one of the notes prepared by M.D. Mistry.

To be sure, while working for the mandals, ambitions, intentions, motivations and idealism have sometimes changed along the way. Some mandal leaders who started well, fighting strongly against injustice and exploitation, themselves became corrupt and exploitative once they got control over more resources and new organizations; others lost interest and became less active and involved; still others looked for bigger and larger organizations and their interest in the mandals became secondary. But some, like Mithibor and Poshina leaders, have continued to work through the mandals tirelessly.

Training of Members and Leaders

OXFAM has helped in organizing nearly fifteen training camps. In most of these *shibirs* participants came from several groups. Two of these *shibirs*, one at Poshina in 1984 and one at Zalod nearly four years ago, were only for members of the respective groups. Some are statewide camps wherein leaders of all mandals are invited to participate; and most generally do participate. In some cases the *shibirs* are for groups of a particular area like the Dharampur *shibir*, or the recently held *shibir* in Dungarpur district of Rajasthan in August 1984, in which groups from several districts of Rajasthan and Sabarkantha district of Gujarat participated. In all of these *shibirs* educated, urbanized, outside activists and concerned academicians are invited. The organizers of the *shibirs* decide which outsiders to invite on the basis of their own information and preferences, and mutual consultation.

The *shibirs* are organized in villages, mainly at ashramshalas, and are very low-cost affairs. Fiften to twenty people live in one hall; the village usually has no electricity and sometimes even the water supply is limited. The food is very simple and only on the last day is a sweet dish served. A six-day *shibir* with more than 100 participants held at Kanjetha village in June 1984, cost only Rs. 21,000 which included lodging, board, travel, material preparation and distribution. The schedule of two sessions, before and after lunch, fill up the whole day and usually continue well beyond dusk. Sometimes participants meet informally at night in small groups and sometimes regular general sessions are also held at night. The groups draw up plans of action both at formal and informal gatherings. Thus the decision to form a district-wide federation type association of village groups in Panchmahals was taken at the *shibir* organized in Isri-Kundol in the winter of 1982. Most of these inter-group *shibirs* register an attendance of between seventy to 100, consisting mostly of leaders, i.e., presidents, secretaries, and treasurers. Ordinary members attend these inter-district statewide *shibirs* in very limited numbers.

Besides these *shibirs*, OXFAM has given grants for eighteen leaders from selected groups to visit other projects in Maharashtra and Gujarat. Some members of women's groups were also sent for training to SEWA (Self Employed Women's Association) at Ahmedabad.

Most of these *shibirs,* except the one held for learning account-keeping and some administrative matters in earlier years, are general wherein issues of the rural poor are discussed.

The normal pattern is for the group members to narrate their experiences, followed by questions and some discussions. Attempts are made to relate the experiences to more generalized issues of social, economic, political and administrative systems. Some of the larger issues discussed are: politicians, political parties and political processes, economic structure in the village situation, caste and class relationships, new policies in regard to forests, loans, credits, subsidies etc.

Generally, sessions are chaired by one person who moderates, usually an outside activist or academician. During the 1984 *shibir* at Kanjetha, an attempt was made to have some of the group leaders, including a female leader from a women's group, in the chair. The move was not very successful, perhaps because they did not know in advance what exactly they were supposed to do as chairpersons, as also because of the inability of the outsiders in restraining themselves from conducting the sessions.

I have attended seven of these training camps and my assessment and suggestions are as follows:

1. These *shibirs* have made a very useful contribution in that they have exposed the leaders to other groups, outsiders and to larger issues.
2. The participants have acquired useful information and knowledge; they have learnt, or at least heard of skills and strategies used by others.
3. They see others with similar problems and difficulties and know that there are many more people like them, as also

outsiders who are involved and concerned. They feel heartened and encouraged. This also builds up their confidence.

4. The *shibirs* provide an invaluable opportunity for them to interact among themselves and with outsiders. Some of the group members, for instance, visited Ahmedabad for the first time. At these *shibirs* for the first time they spoke publicly to large groups.

5. As they narrate their experiences, the very process of narration helps them to analyze and understand their activities and the larger environment.

6. Reportedly, some of them were inspired to take up struggle and confrontation-oriented activities after attending these *shibirs*.

7. More importantly, I think it has been a worthwhile exposure for the outside academicians and activists. Some of them were, for the first time, exposed to such groups, and to the idea of weaker sections generating and managing these type of activities by themselves. My impression is that many of them, for the first time, also understood the problems and difficulties that these groups face as also their skills and capabilities. In my experience of discussing these groups with outside (urban) activists and academicians, I have found that they either get very excited and euphoric about the small groups phenomenon or very disappointed and pessimistic when they see the groups not measuring up to their expectations. The *shibirs* perhaps help them to understand the small groups in their proper perspective. The *shibirs* have begun the process of helping to build the bridge between the general and the specific, knowledge and activity, outsiders and insiders, rural and urban.

8. These *shibirs* are however getting repetitive. The same people narrate the same experiences, raise the same questions and discuss the same issues.

9. While there is much exchange of information and exposure, how much internalization takes place is something that has not been assessed. There is not any attempt to explore the ways of translating the information into action.

10. This is because it is assumed that exchange of experiences would automatically lead to analysis and learning for action.

Outsiders tend to get euphoric about the *shibirs* because the experience is novel and unusual for them. It is rare to find members of the weaker sections, some of them barely literate and dressed in tattered clothes, standing up and speaking before a gathering of 100 or more people. This is so striking that one tends to get carried away by it.

11. While larger questions are raised and even an attempt is made to relate them with the micro-experiences that are brought out, neither are alternatives for macro-issues nor action-plans for micro-situations developed.

12. The gatherings are generally too large and methods adopted too weak to provide any intensive learning that can be taken up for action by various groups.

13. Also, enough spade work is not undertaken before organizing the *shibirs*. No method other than the seminar method, and no other aids are used. Nor is any systematic and rigorous assessment done after the *shibirs* conclude.

14. While there are reports that some of the group members have taken up social justice activities after attending the *shibirs*, no systematic follow up exercise has been done so far. I do not think that participation in the *shibirs* have made any noticeable difference for those groups which are stagnant or are disintegrating.

15. Since there are many groups that are now two to five years old and whose leaders have attended at least five to six *shibirs* of the same type, it is now time to have more planned and intensive 'workshop' type *shibirs*.

16. Such *shibirs* should be small with twenty to thirty participants. Besides seminar type discussions, sessions of group exercises in which attempts are made to translate experiences into action should be included. It should provide opportunities for the participants to do more rigorous self-assessment (of one's groups), identify gaps and needs, and to develop plans and strategies.[4]

17. It is also necessary to have *shibirs* for ordinary members who are not leaders.

[4] SETU organized a consultation meeting of resource persons in December 1984 to develop a programme of training and followed it up with a week's training programme in October 1985. However, this was not continued.

18. In my view, Gujarat, as yet, has not developed capabilities for the training of activists from the grass-roots. Men, methods and materials are lacking. I doubt whether even the outside activists—those who are educated, working with established voluntary agencies or movements, and know these areas and their problems—can straightaway fill this role. Even they will need preparation for the role.

19. Various types of training need to be organized. For instance, *shibirs* for internal management, accounting and records, management of economic activities and getting and managing government sponsored programmes may be organized. *Shibirs* on interaction and networking among the groups may be organized. *Shibirs* may be necessary to diagnose the participatory and social action activities. *Shibirs* for learning skills in communication—songs, dance, drama, puppetry etc., would be useful. *Shibirs* can be held for resource persons. *Shibirs* can be organized by some groups themselves, through half-day visits to each other. The *shibirs* of the present type are also necessary, and should not be entirely abandoned.

20. *Shibirs* are a very effective and powerful vehicle. *Shibirs* held so far have performed very useful functions of awareness, exposure, getting together, interaction and inspiration. What is suggested here is a more intensive, systematic and well-organized effort.

5

Activities: Economic and Developmental

The small groups are involved in various types of activities. These can broadly be categorized as: (*a*) economic activities; (*b*) social action and conscientization activities; (*c*) educational and social reform activities; and (*d*) general developmental and facilitating activities. Quite a few groups have been active and instrumental in starting new and separate organizations. These are the spin-offs from their mandals based on their initiative and efforts to generate more benefits for their communities through the government's schemes, projects and programmes. Some mandals take an active interest in political matters but these shall be dealt with separately when we discuss the relationship of these mandals with the outside world.

Economic Activities

All the groups are engaged in economic activities. In fact, that has been the starting point for many groups. The economic activities are mainly related to agriculture: loans for seeds, fertilizers, well-deepening, -blasting or -repairs, well-irrigation through machines, lift-irrigation, soil conservation and buying bullocks and buffaloes. Some groups have also advanced loans to members or to other groups for bamboo work, broom-making, for making grinding stones, for making bowls and dinner plates of leaves (generally used for group dinners), *bidi* (Indian cigarettes) rolling etc. All cooperative societies supported by OXFAM, except the Tembda Cooperative in Sabarkantha district, are involved in non-agricultural activities like bamboo work, dairy, grain-shop, etc.

The economic activities are mainly based on OXFAM funds, but all cooperative societies have also got financial help from the government. Groups like Gamdi, Zalod, Abhlod, Kundawada in

Panchmahals, and Mota Kantharia, Vanta, Isri-Kundol, Chuna-khan in Sabarkantha have taken up some economic activities directly under their own mandals with help from various government schemes. Gamdi and Zalod have got subsidies from the government for bullocks; Mota Kantharia has started Ambar Charka activity through the help of a Sarvodaya voluntary organization; Vanta Mandal organized a food-for-work programme; Jamran group has taken up brick-kiln activity. It should be noted that here we are not considering economic activities started by the initiative and efforts of the mandals by forming a separate organization. These will be discussed later in the chapter. The economic activities of nearly five groups in Panchmahals and six groups in Sabarkantha are entirely based on OXFAM funds.

One reason why some groups have not been able to start economic activities other than those funded by OXFAM is the bureaucracy's lack of understanding of the legal status and formal structure of these groups. The only organizations of the people that the bureaucracy is familiar and comfortable with are elected panchayats, registered cooperatives, or government sponsored organizations for specific programmes like the Small Farmers' Development Agency. Government officials are sometimes not able to understand what these mandals are, and how the people have organized on their own through a structure other than co-operative societies for economic activities. They were not sure about the legal status of these mandals and whether it was safe for them to officially channel economic programmes through them. Both Gamdi and Zalod mandals received subsidies for bullocks and the mandals advanced loans for this purpose to their members. But later on a technical issue was raised—whether the government can subsidize loans advanced by a group that is neither a cooperative society nor a bank.

If the groups are to take up the government's economic development programmes, they will have to be officially recognized by the taluk and district level administration. Efforts need to be made at the state level for such recognition.

The choice of taking up a particular economic activity is made by the groups themselves. They are generally well aware of the economic needs of their communities and activities that need to be promoted. That is why they are able to make precise requests for funds to OXFAM, be they for seeds, fertilizers, bullocks, improvement of wells or bunding.

The decision about advancing loans—the amount and the loanees—is taken in different ways. Some call a general meeting while others such as Isri-Kundol form falia-wise or hamlet-wise committees. The committee members make enquiries and then recommend the loanees. Considerable care is generally taken to ensure that loans are advanced to poor farmers and not to the well-to-do. But if, as sometimes happen, mandal leaders themselves are greedy this criterion is not followed. From a very general and unsystematic observation it seems that groups in the Isri-Kundol area of Sabarkantha have tended to give loans to well-to-do farmers also. These are the groups which have more leaders having government jobs and some of them owning at least 10 acres of land.

Thus Mota Kantharia, Isri-Kundol, Chhitadara, Kagda Mahuda have all advanced loans to farmers, including executive committee members, who are not the poorest in the community. But it should be noted that even these mandals, with the exception of Chhitadara, have also advanced loans to very small and marginal farmers whose holdings are one to three acres only. The Chhitadara mandal, which has received as much as Rs. 40,000 as funds from OXFAM and which has the lowest membership among all the mandals has advanced loans for machines to only eight members. They are farmers owning at least seven acres of land and having wells and electricity connections on their farms. When asked how beneficiaries were selected the Chhitadara mandal replied that since they had asked OXFAM for funds for electric machines and since only nine farmers had electric connections on their farms, they had no option but to give loans only to these farmers. Though they claim that these are all marginal farmers, our inquiries revealed that if all the land they own or cultivate is put together, their holdings would exceed the limits of marginal landholdings.

The groups face another problem in advancing loans to the very poor. Their very poverty makes their chances of returning the loans slim. Jalampur and Poshina, for instance, take into consideration the possibility of recovering the loan based not only on the economic criterion but also on the honesty of the applicant concerned. They try to judge the applicant's behaviour, his past record and what they call his *swabhav*[1] (character) before

---

[1] Literally translated it would mean natural tendency.

advancing the loan. The experience of advancing loans to the very marginal people has not been encouraging. In the case of Sabarkantha, as mentioned earlier, the Thakardas themselves admit of both the inability and unwillingness of 'our people to return the money.' Even a group like Gamdi in Panchmahals, which is quite active and which took the initiative in advancing loans to the scheduled caste members and members of another very backward caste called vadi, did not have a positive experience. Here the scheduled caste members were advanced loans for bamboo work. They were to pay back Rs. 10 per week, but after the first few weeks they stopped repayment. Vadis, a nomadic tribe, who were advanced a loan of Rs. 100 per member for making grinding stones, have also not repaid any money.

There are groups where even adivasi members have not repaid loans regularly. Ensuring repayment of loans is generally a bothersome task for leaders of the groups. Most group leaders reported that they had to make very vigorous efforts to get repayments. Exerting pressure would spoil their relationship with community members. They lose members who are defaulters. The defaulters simply drop out, stop all interactions with the group and sometimes may even go round criticizing the group. The groups also refrain from taking any legal measures.[2] (It is not clear whether they can take any legal measure as they are neither cooperative societies nor banks, nor are they advancing loans under any government programmes.)

We found that the loan recovery position of three groups in Sabarkantha and three groups in Panchmahals is very bad; that of three groups in Sabarkantha and five groups in Panchmahals is substantially good (though they have nearly 30 to 50 per cent defaulters); and that of nearly five groups is excellent. The Vanta group in Sabarkantha, for instance, has revolved its money seven times out of a loan fund of Rs. 10,000. The Chunakhan and Kagda Mahuda groups has nearly 100 per cent recovery. Mithibor, a group in a very backward area and with uneducated and inexperienced leadership has more than 80 per cent recovery.

However, the leaders of these groups (except when they themselves are defaulters) are generally very anxious about the recovery of loans and make sustained efforts in that direction. In some cases they have formed street-wise committees, in others they have

---

[2] At the time of advancing loans the loanees have to sign a promissory note.

designated each executive member with the responsibility of recovering a number of loans. A few groups have appointed paid
workers (mostly from among their own members) who recover
loans on a commission basis. For instance, Gamdi group pays four
per cent (out of the five per cent surplus they charge to the loanee)
to the member who is assigned the work of recovery. There are
four major reasons for the difficulty faced by the groups in recovery
of loans:

1. The mandal leaders themselves may be greedy and dishonest.
2. The loanees, particularly the very small and marginal farmers, are not able to produce enough surplus to repay the
   loans on time. Their total production, even with the inputs
   bought from the loan, remains so meagre that vagaries of
   weather or any accident (and their agriculture is highly
   accident-prone) often does not leave them with any surplus
   at all. For instance, the monsoons in 1981 and 1982 were
   very bad and that affected the recovery of most groups.
3. Most farmers have been chronically and habitually in debt.
   So when they have a little bit of surplus and if the choice is
   between spending the money on some personal or social
   need and repayment of the instalment, they tend to do the
   former. Generally, expenditure on social occasions—deaths,
   marriages, religious rituals—takes priority over repayment
   of debts.
4. The experience of the last nearly thirty years has shown
   farmers that public debts are soft. Under the entire cooperative movement and a number of other development programmes it has been possible for them to use loans for
   personal purposes because nobody monitors them. If corrupt
   officials are paid their dues they do not care about proper
   use or timely recovery. In spite of defaulting for many years
   nothing has happened to them. They are also aware that for
   political reasons government loans are often written off. So
   they hope that credit advanced by their groups would similarly be written off.

The president of Chunakhan group had this to say about recovery
of loans:

Whatever amount our mandal has loaned has been recovered. But for this we have faced a lot of difficulties. Even if people earn more because of our loans they do not repay regularly. Often, the office bearers have to go to their houses or write notes to the loanees. The 'old class' does not believe in repayment whether it is government money or OXFAM money. The young people consider it as mandal's money, and mandal's activity and, therefore, consider repayment an absolute duty. That is why big tension exists between the two generations.

However, the leaders have understood that if the groups cannot recover loans they would disintegrate, because they would lose credibility. The constant hammering by the OXFAM Field Officer, his uncompromising, tough and unrelenting attitude[3] whenever he finds financial mismanagement or lethargy of the leaders in recovery of loans has also kept them on their toes. Some groups are very vigilant and strict about it. They normally do not give another loan to a defaulter unless they are convinced that the reasons were genuine and that repayment will be made. Kagda Mahuda in Sabarkantha has introduced a system of fines. The defaulters have to repay Rs. 130 instead of the regular Rs. 110 for every Rs. 100 of the loan.

The groups have an excellent record in the utilization of loans, unlike the experience of credit through public institutions where the incidence of misuse is very high. The leaders of the groups are on the spot. They take considerable pains to see that the loans are used for the declared purposes and not for personal, social or religious purposes. They insist that family members of the loanee should get down to the work when the loans are given for a purpose requiring labour, like well-deepening or bunding. Teams formed by the group go to the spot, measure the work done, or climb down the wells and satisfy themselves. Sometimes they give money in instalments on the basis of the progress of the work.

Quite a few groups revolve their funds by loaning to different members after the first round of loans are recovered. For instance, Kagda Mahuda revolved its funds four times between July 1980 to April 1983 and extended it to 199 beneficiaries. Gamdi revolved its

[3] His efforts and some incidents are described in OXFAM notes, Appendix II.

fund for bullocks twice. Vanta mandal which received the first
OXFAM loan of Rs. 5,000 in 1981, revolved it three times between
1981 and 1983. The second loan of Rs. 5,000 received in July 1982,
was revolved twice between 1982 and 1983. By 1984 it had revolved
its loans seven times. In the process, it generated additional funds
for itself, and by 1984, it had collected Rs. 5,000 of its own for
repayment to OXFAM. However, circulating loans is mainly possible in case of onetime activities like bunding, well-deepening,
loans for bullocks and buffaloes. It is difficult in case of seeds and
fertilizers where the beneficiaries need loans repeatedly.

It is expected that eventually the groups will become financially
self-sufficient by generating enough funds to carry on small scale
economic activities on their own after returning the OXFAM
funds. But the record of generating their own funds is so far not
very encouraging.

Groups have adopted several ways to generate their own funds.
Firstly, there are the annual membership fees. But these are
meagre; sometimes as low as Re. 1. Besides, there is considerable
irregularity in paying membership fees. Many groups have not
collected these fees more than once. The fund so collected is so
meagre that, at best, it can take care of their administrative
expenses—travel, stationery, audit fees etc.

Secondly, a few groups, we came across only six such, charge an
additional 5 to 10 per cent on the loans advanced. If the repayment
is regular, this generates a regular income of between Rs. 1,000 to
Rs. 4,000 a year. But sometimes this creates a problem for the
group leaders. If this method is adopted only in the second or third
year, then members accuse the leaders, of favouring the first batch
to whom no surplus was charged. They derive their justification
from the fact that quite a few of the first batch loanees were
generally family members, relatives or friends of the leaders. The
Vantda Milk Cooperative faced this problem when they started
charging 6 per cent surplus to the second and subsequent batches.
The reason for the first batch loanees being close to the leaders
was because initially, they could only mobilize people they knew.
Also, with time they came up with newer ideas. The first year they
were anxious to get the activities going and did not give much
thought to generating funds. Sometimes members question the
propriety of charging interest. Members of the Navavenpur group
questioned its president why they should pay any interest on the
loans when OXFAM was not charging any interest.

Thirdly, some groups undertake income generating activities like renting out diesel pumps for drawing water from the wells. Gamdi has been doing this. It has, however, not been very profitable. Gamdi had to pay a yearly instalment of Rs. 2,000 to OXFAM on this machine. As their profit was not very high they had to request OXFAM to convert the loan into a grant. Gamdi, Abhlod and Zalod groups had also tried to generate some funds by sponsoring lotteries but were not very successful. Chhitadara organized a film show and collected Rs. 600.

The group leaders are aware that the outside activists would like them to be financially independent and self-sufficient. They have heared them say this repeatedly, in private, in public speeches and in their writings. Therefore, when asked in formal situations or public gatherings like the *shibirs*, they proclaim that they would generate their own funds. But in informal person to person situations most of them admit that it is very difficult for them to generate enough funds from their own people to make the groups financially self-sufficient.

For instance, when I asked when they had to repay the OXFAM loans they were quite ambivalent in their responses. While they have signed agreements and are aware of it, some of them tried to hint that OXFAM should, or would, give them more time. Some of them were also hoping, because of a couple of such examples that they have heard of from other groups, that OXFAM might convert the loans into grants. The president of the Margala group, who heroically proclaimed during the *shibir* at Kanjetha that they would be successful in returning the loans, urged us on the same evening, and also earlier during our field visit, to get OXFAM to convert at least part of the loan into a grant.

Development Activities

A majority of the groups are involved in getting the benefits of the government's development programmes to their village. Twenty-one of the groups show a more intensive involvement in these activities and a willingness to undertake and implement the programmes.

Some of the new organizations could be started by the groups as a result of their successful efforts to pull down towards them the benefits of government programmes and facilities like roads, electricity, telephones, eucalyptus saplings from the forest department, and benefits of TRYSEM, IRDP, and tribal sub-plan.

Besides, several groups act as facilitators in helping their community members to get the benefits of government programmes. They help them with information about where to go and what to do, procure application forms for them from government offices, accompany them to various offices, follow up their cases and if necessary, fight and confront the local bureaucracy.

On the other hand, they also willingly come forward when the government wants to do some work in their villages, by helping the concerned department to identify beneficiaries, putting them in touch with people, persuading the people to respond, pinpointing suitable locations and providing hospitality.

Some selected examples of groups that have taken up such activities are given below:

A. *Gamdi Group*:
   1. Obtained forms for TB patients, had them duplicated and got a stipend of Rs. 100 per month for them under a Social Welfare Board scheme.
   2. People were given information about the schemes of the District Industries Centre and application forms were brought and distributed to the people for undertaking cottage industries.
   3. People were given information and guidance about the Antyodaya Scheme. Forms were printed by the group. Forty-three applications for goats, bullocks and housing were made and followed up with the government. Eighteen people were benefited.
   4. Under the Twenty Point Programme, five members of the group had got sanction for housing. The government officials had taken bribes and stopped the second instalment when they found out that the members had complained to the mandal. Their cases were taken up to the ministerial level by the group. The amount they had paid as bribes were returned and the instalments were released.

B. *Isri-Kundol Group*:
   1. Procured buffaloes for ten members.
   2. Undertook supervision work of one balwadi started by a voluntary agency in the village.
   3. Organized meetings to discuss the proposed Forest Bill of the central government.

C. *Mota Kantharia Group*:
1. Helped twenty-nine individuals to get buffaloes under the Tribal Sub-Plan.
2. Prepared papers for getting sewing machines for seven people from the District Industries Centre.
3. Under the Amber Charkha Scheme, seventy-five amber-charkhas have been acquired for as many members of the community.

D. *Chunakhan Group*:
1. It succeeded in getting the following facilities for the village: electricity, water-works, balwadi, approach road and public telephone.

E. *Vanta Group*:
1. Helped villagers to fill up forms for getting subsidies under various schemes.
2. Helped people to get land transferred to their names in case of father's death or division of property.

F. *Abhlod Group*:
1. Helped forty-seven farmers get subsidy for bullocks under SRDP.
2. During irrigation canal work, the PWD staff was helped to transport its machines; was provided hospitality, night shelter, place for storing equipment, and extra labourers to finish the work speedily.

Spin-off

Several groups wanted to expand their developmental and economic activities. They felt that it would be better to do it separately and independently of the group. One reason is the legal status of the group which is that of a public trust or society, while most economic activities involving government funds are usually channeled through the structure of the cooperative societies. Also, the cooperative movement is relatively better and stronger in the state, and groups seem to prefer the cooperative format. Secondly, major activities require more funds and facilities like buildings, furnishings and staff, therefore, they are better managed by a more structured organization. The mandals have a loose and flexible organization. It leaves the group free to take on more mobilizational and social action type of activities without harming or inviting trouble for activities where they have got resources from the government.

Some of the villages where these groups function, already had schools or cooperatives. But some institutions came about as spin-off from the groups activities and by the conscious and organized efforts of the group members. While these are separate institutions they are controlled and managed by the groups.

At the time of this study, four groups in Sabarkantha and three groups in Panchmahals had started new institutions. Some examples are:

A. *Tembda*
   1. Milk Cooperative.
B. *Isri-Kundol*
   1. Milk Cooperative
   2. Educational Trust for a higher secondary school
   3. Hostel for boys
C. *Abhlod*
   1. Branch of the Agricultural Credit Cooperative
   2. Irrigation Cooperative
   3. Poultry Cooperative
   4. School
D. *Gamdi*
   1. Irrigation Cooperative
   2. Poultry Cooperative
   3. Brick Producers' Cooperative
   4. Milk Cooperative
   5. Agricultural Credit Cooperative

Implications of Economic and Developmental Activities

1. It is doubtful whether economic activities on such a small scale would ever (even in the long run) bring the poor above subsistence level. The inputs through loans that mandals give are small and sporadic. They would need more inputs, for which they have to depend on others, if their incomes and production are to rise.

   Their landholdings and economic capabilities are at such a low level that any accident: bad monsoon, crop-theft, cutting or burning because of internal feuds (which are common), pushes them back to where they were before getting assistance from the mandal. After all, some of these people had received loans from credit cooperatives earlier but it had not made much difference to their economic conditions or release them from their chronic indebtedness.

2. At the same time, financial help from the group has given them tremendous economic and social relief, though temporary.

   a. For very poor members any increase in production, though not enough to pull them out of subsistence, has been sufficient to give them enough food, a little better clothing and some additional necessities of life.

   b. In case of drought, sometimes, they would face near starvation or would have to mortgage whatever little assets they have. Help by the mandal has provided critical relief. It has helped prevent them from being pushed further into the depths of poverty and becoming totally destitute.

   c. If it is a question of the survival of the bottom 20 per cent of the population, as some argue, economic activity by the groups is helping them in this survival.

   d. There is a lot of flexibility in the mandal's economic help. In a crisis people can get help almost overnight; there are no papers and procedures; no repeated visits to taluk and district offices; and no bribes, commissions and insults. This in itself is a great relief for people who would otherwise have to go through the tortuous and circuitous routes of getting loans from government and public institutions.

   e. It has also helped them to save the time they had to spend in procuring inputs. For instance, the Thuris of Gambhoi and Vantda who manage the bamboo cooperatives have found great relief due to their cooperative's economic activity. Earlier, each individual had to go to the market in town to buy bamboos. Besides costing him nearly three to four times more than it does now, the entire transaction also took a whole day. Now he mostly gets the bamboo delivered to him at his home.

f. Going to purchase the bamboos individually would often mean ill-treatment and sometimes misbehaviour towards their women. All of them agreed that their women have got considerable relief because of their group's economic activity. Similarly the members of the Vantda Milk Cooperative reported that before they started their cooperative they had to go to a nearby town twice a day to sell their milk to another cooperative and they always got cheated on fat count.

g. Some of the groups in Dangs and Dharampur where drinking water was a severe problem have constructed wells. Earlier, women had to walk several kilometers to fetch water and they were able to bring only two pots of water a day. Besides facing severe hardship it also prevented them from going to work. In summer when streams and rivulets dried up people had to go without baths for weeks together. Now, with wells in their villages, women have got considerable relief.

3. In Sabarkantha and Panchmahals, economic activities of the groups have relieved many poor farmers of debt to private money-lenders. Since many of the small farmers had stopped getting credit from cooperatives because of non-repayment of loans, they had again reverted to private money-lenders. Gamdi group for instance, was able to get back ninety-six acres of mortgaged land belonging to fifty-six farmers. And till 1984 only three of the fifty-six farmers had remortgaged their land.

4. Gamdi, Abhlod and Mithibor groups reported that seasonal migration, in search of work, from their villages was reduced considerably.

5. Economic activities with limited funds sometimes tend to make the groups close and exclusive. We have noted that in case of some Sabarkantha groups there has been a distinct reluctance to include the Thakardas. Jalampur group, for instance, has not admitted new members in spite of applications because they had only limited funds to distribute. Lavaria group in Panchmahals also had reservations about taking new members because, according to the president, now that we have funds, selfish people are coming forward '

6. Because groups have money to manage and distribute, sometimes ill-feeling and distrust are generated between members and leaders and between the leaders themselves. Because of their past experiences people are worried and distrustful when money is involved. Their risk capability is very low or nil and, therefore, the level of their distrust is high. That is why groups are finding it difficult to get contributions from their members. Even groups like Gamdi and Abhlod where many economic and social developmental activities are generated, and where practically every household in the village and many households in the villages within their area of activity have benefited, fund raising from the members has been a problem. The president of Abhlod felt that if he pressurized the villagers to become members or to give more funds he would lose their trust. Yet, at one time they had collected considerable funds for building a temple.

7. It seems that these communities have yet to accept the idea of pooling their resources for a secular community activity, unless they see a direct, immediate and tangible benefit. Tribals in Panchmahals, for instance, spend between Rs. 2,000 to 25,000 on a marriage. In Poshina, tribals may easily mobilize as much as Rs. 25,000 to, what they call, 'revenge' the tribals of another village. Most tribal communities seem to spend freely and sometimes lavishly on social and religious matters. Recently, in Abhlod and Vangad area villages, people collected several thousands to give to a member of the Legislative Assembly, who is also their religious leader, for constructing a temple in Rajasthan. But generally, they do not come forward as readily to contribute to the mandal's activities. Perhaps they need time to appreciate the benefits of the groups' work for them in order to contribute easily and spontaneously. Perhaps intensive and vigorous conscientization efforts from outsiders and at inter-community levels may be necessary.

8. Groups which have only or mainly concentrated on economic activities do not seem to be very active, and are not growing, or making much impact on their communities. Groups like Lambadia, Mota Kantharia, Chitadara,

Navavenpur in Sabarkantha and Nagvav and Margala in Panchmahals have mainly concentrated on economic activities; their impact on the life of the communities is not visible and they themselves seem to be stagnating.

9. Yet economic activities are pivotal for every group. If they have no economic activities then they would not have any locus standi in their communities. It is highly doubtful whether they will be able to undertake any social and conscientization activities or even survive unless they undertake some economic activities.

10. Developmental activities, some of which are economic in nature, help the groups to increase their credibility with their own communities.

11. These help them to extend themselves beyond the group members as here they try to help any community member who is needy.

12. These activities are tangible and concrete and help the community members to realize the strength and importance of the mandals.

13. The mandal leaders and sometimes other members learn to interact with local bureaucracy and gain in skills and confidence in managing developmental activities.

14. At the same time these developmental activities, particularly starting new organizations, take considerable time and energy. They also involve compromises and manipulations which undermine the ethos of the mandals.

15. The resources and infrastructure that go with these institutions like offices, furniture, travel expenses money and employees, tend to change the styles and behaviour of mandal leaders who manage them. They tend to think and behave like 'leaders' and a certain distancing from the poor in the community begins to take place.

16. They tend to behave more like the political representatives of their communities who occupy positions in political and public institutions dispensing favours and distributing benefits.

17. Because they spend more time in these administratively more structured institutions, the mandal's activities, particularly mobilizational, awareness, social justice and anti-corruption activities, tend to be at a low ebb.

6

Activities: Social Action, Social Reform and Awareness

Social Action and Conscientization

A very active leader of a small group from South Gujarat, one who helped form several other groups in the neighbouring villages, narrated the following incident at the *shibir* held at Kanjetha in the summer of 1984:

> First we started groups in three villages then expanded to five villages. The *sarpanch* of one of the villages thought that his power was being curtailed because of these groups. He started intimidating and threatening us and other members. He tried to create factions. But the village people got together and sent him away. The *sarpanch* realized the power of the group and apologized the next day.
>
> Our teachers (of primary schools) were headstrong, formed cliques, went hunting, held big parties, got drunk and misbehaved. Anybody who tried to restrain them was bullied and beaten up.
>
> We started performing dramas[1] on this. The whole village would get together, sometimes as many as 3,000 to 4,000 people from nearby villages would gather to watch. This created a lot of impact. The teachers have been exposed and are now better behaved.

Another group leader, a twenty-six year old tribal with high school education, from the same district, narrated the following experience:

[1] There is a folk-tradition in this area of performing *Tamashas* (folk-plays).

I have a very interesting story to tell you. But for that I must introduce its hero first. The hero rules my district single-handedly.

He is: President, District Panchayat;
President, Village Forest Cooperative;
President, District Forest Cooperatives Union;
President, Milk Producers' Cooperative Society;
President, District Youth Congress-I
President, District Board of State Transport; and
President, District Gun Holders' Committee.

His family members and relatives occupy all other positions in the district. Anybody who contests an election against him or his men will be intimidated by his goondas who would point a gun at his head and force him to withdraw. In the village panchayat election his brother-in-law was contesting. We put up a candidate against him. Our candidate was threatened by his men with guns. The candidate lost courage and withdrew.

The Forest Cooperative Society of our village, of which he is a president, was singled out and members were not given loans and subsidies, while members of other forest cooperatives received loans and subsidies. When we asked the president the reason for this, he replied that since our cooperative had to spend heavily on constructing the office and storage, no loans could be advanced.

At about that time the general body meeting of the forest society was held. We talked to the people; it was being discussed that the president had misappropriated a lot of money. The office and storage could not cost even Rs. 2,00,000 but Rs. 9,00,000 had been shown as the expenditure. We mobilized a lot of members to attend the general body meeting. The president had also come to know about the grumbling among the people, and that we had mobilized people to attend the meeting. As he was expecting fireworks at the meeting he had also brought the MLA, the Registrar of the Cooperative Society, the President of the Education Committee of the District Panchayat, the Bank Manager and several other officers to overawe the people. Although according to rules the agenda and accounts have to be sent a week in advance, it was distributed only at the time of the meeting, and before people could read them the meeting proceeded with the work.

When the meeting began, I asked, 'According to the bye-laws you were supposed to circulate the agenda and accounts one week in advance. Why did you not circulate it in advance?' The president said, 'The press was closed. We could not get it printed in time.' I asked, 'Were all the presses in Gujarat closed?' People started laughing. The president stared at me and proceeded, 'The building that we have constructed has cost Rs. 9,00,000. Do you approve?'

People attending the meeting started murmuring their objections and gestured to each other to get up and speak. So I got up and asked him, 'Why was another building constructed when there was already one in the nearby village? Moreover, the expenditure of Rs. 9,00,000 for the building is too high. Can you show the papers and vouchers?' The president said, 'Yes. Come to the society's office. Everything will be shown.' I asked, 'Don't we have a right to see it here?'

People started making a noise. Some said everything should be cleared here and now. At this juncture the Chairman of the District Education Committee thought that he must help out the president. He angrily said, 'You have no manners. Because you have got education, you have become arrogant. But people gathered here are not stupid. They will not be swayed by you.'

I: 'Before taking the decision of constructing the building did you pass a resolution by the executive committee?'

President: 'Yes.'

I: 'Would the members of the executive committee come on the stage and admit that?'

President: 'Yes.'

I: 'Committee members please come on to the stage.'

But nobody came. Meanwhile a few of the president's cronies got up and started heckling. The meeting was disrupted.

In Dharampur taluk a member of the Sabarsingi group reported that in his village the teacher of the primary school never turned up and the school remained closed. When several petitions to the education department remained unanswered, the youth organization decided to take direct action. They published a pamphlet, threatened satyagraha and broke open the school lock. The teacher came and attended school. He sought a transfer after two months and the new teacher is now regularly attending school.[2]

Bhaljibhai, president of the Mithibor group, a twenty-four year old youth with education up to seventh grade, prepared a list of farmers who had to mortgage their land to the local Vora[3] traders against very small loans several years ago and sent it to the district collector who instituted an inquiry. In turn, the Vora traders accused Bhaljibhai of theft and filed a false case against him. To break his morale and to provide a deterrent to others the police handcuffed him, tied him with ropes and paraded him through the village.

In the same village the group took up the issue of mortgaged land of four tribals. The local trader had planted eucalyptus trees on that land and the saplings had been obtained in the name of the tribal owners of the land. As a tactic, the group kept quiet for a while to let the trees grow and then moved the court to get back possession of the land and the trees. The money-lender sensed trouble and gave up his claims to the trees as also the land.

The Mithibor group, in its short period of activity, had to take up several such issues because it is a very backward area located in the interior of a forested and hilly region. It has fought success-fully against the harrassment and extortions of the police and forest staff and against the exploitation of traders.

The Zalod group has carried out many struggles to assert their rights. They fought for getting minimum wages for the road con-struction workers and forced the contractor to pay them wages in the daytime and in a group, rather than at night and individually. Some of the group leaders, along with leaders of other neigh-bouring groups, organized a mass procession and a rally against the statewide anti-reservation movement. The rally brought together nearly 5,000 adivasis. Another protest rally and a mass meeting was organized against the forest bill of the government.

Several groups in Panchmahals got together to organize a major rally in collaboration with the Rashtriya Congress Party to voice their grievances about the many problems that adivasis faced and

[2] All the above three incidents are abridged and translated from Joseph Makwan's report on 'The Kanjetha Shibir,' Ahmedabad: SETU (Centre for Know-ledge and Action), August 1984. The author participated in the *shibir* and had listened to these experiences.

[3] Belonging to the Muslim trading community of that name.

against the government's inaction. The lead was taken by the president of the Lavaria group.

Two groups, Vangad and Poshina published pamphlets giving information about minimum wages and exhorting the adivasis not to pay bribes for loans and subsidies. Poshina group of Sabarkantha had to even confront landowners who threatened them and refused to give work to the labourers.

Gamdi and Abhlod had to carry out satyagraha for regularizing the bus service to their villages. Groups have successfully moved inefficient or corrupt bureaucracies to get telephones, roads, irrigation, subsidies and loans. Sometimes applications, frequent visits and meetings with government officials; and at other times exerting pressure on politicians at taluk, district or state level; have yielded desired results. As a last resort they threaten agitation which they carry out if it becomes necessary.

Many groups have fought against the corruption of individual bureaucrats at local levels. The Vangad group claims having got seven *talatis* (revenue clerks) transferred. Abhlod, Gamdi, Mithibor, Lavaria, Zalod, all have similar incidents to report about *talatis*, police, forest guards, state transport drivers, village level workers, health workers etc. Gamdi, for instance, found a health worker selling malaria tablets, meant to be distributed free in the village, when the village was in the grip of malaria and five children had died. The group contacted the police, got the health worker's house raided and a case was filed against him. He was eventually dismissed. The new health worker regularly disinfected wells and also distributed the medicine.

The Vangad group also fought against a voluntary agency which, according to the group, was not paying minimum wages to the carpet weavers. The voluntary agency finally closed down its centre in the Vangad village.

The Abhlod mandal organized two satyagrahas demanding increase in frequency and regularity of buses. Nearly 500 people participated in the satyagrahas. The Abhlod group also organized a demonstration before the Public Works Department to repair an approach road which was in a very bad condition and was being completely neglected by the PWD. Construction of an irrigation canal in a nearby village had been left incomplete for the last thirty-five years, though on government records it was shown as completed. Many petitions; visits to government offices; contacts with senior government officers and political representatives of the taluk and district; and state level political institutions; ultimately moved the government to take up the work. At the time of our field visit in March 1984 the work had been completed.

The same group carried out a fight against an old established voluntary agency of the district which was running an Ashramshala. They found that the principal and teachers were neglecting their work; attendance of both teachers and students was low; there was corruption in the management of the hostel where students were not given enough and nutritious food. They demanded to check the attendance records and supervize the food given to the students. Finally, they asked the voluntary agency to let them manage the school. They did not succeed in getting control over the school but the management of the school improved. Moreover, the group started its own school with the help of the *Khet Vikas Parishad*, another state level voluntary agency.

At times some mandals have lost government subsidies or loans because they did not know the correct procedures and they refused to bribe the officials. The Isri-Kundol group had completed a well-deepening programme and had then applied to the taluk development office for a subsidy. They were told that since they had not taken prior approval for deepening the wells they were not entitled to the subsidy, unless of course, they paid the bribe. The group preferred to do without the subsidy rather than pay the bribe.

The incidents described here may give an impression that things go smoothly and that it is easy for the group. But it is not at all so. A lot of hard work and tension is involved in preparing a victim to take up an issue. Some of them get scared and back out halfway or let them down at the last minute. These types of activities require repeated visits, fighting against rumours and allegations about their own motives, resisting threats and temptations, putting up with shouting and quarrelling and careful paper work. It requires time and resources, patience and perseverance, courage and commitment, and a willingness to suffer. It also requires tact, strategic planning and skillful handling. And all this the leaders of the mandals have learnt quickly and demonstrated repeatedly.

The campaigns of the mandals against corrupt petty officials have been very successful. In many cases they have been able to get back the money already taken by the officials. Generally all groups, including those who have not taken up social action activities intensively, have reported that they could effectively control the corruption and harassment of *talatis*.[4]

Thus, the corruption of petty officials has been reduced to a great extent in villages where the groups operate. These officials have now learnt to curtail their malpractices in relation to the members of the group and their villages. However, they continue to indulge in corruption in villages where the group's influence has not extended. They look for safer areas, and in some cases, get themselves transferred to a place where they can continue to indulge in their corrupt practices.

Table 9 lists groups with regard to the different types of activities they emphasize. Fourteen of the thirty-eight groups have taken up social action activities often and quite vigorously. Some other groups have also taken up these activities, but sporadically. As Table 9 shows, seven out of eleven groups in Panchmahals and only two out of fifteen groups in Sabarkantha have taken up these activities intensively.

TABLE 9
*Types of Activities**

District/ Taluk	Only or mainly economic activities	Educational & Other Developmental activities	Social Reform Activities	Social Justice & Conscientization activities
Sabarkantha	5	8	3	2
Panchmahals	3	5	4	7
Dharampur	3	8	6	5
Total	11	21	13	14

* Columns in this table are not mutually exclusive. For instance, all groups have taken up economic activities to some extent so groups in the second and subsequent columns are involved in economic activities as well.

Groups in most backward areas, Dangs, Dharampur, Panchmahals and Khedbrahma of Sabarkantha, where there is greater corruption and exploitation have taken up these issues more often.

[4] The harassment by and petty corruption of these revenue clerks is the most widespread and common phenomenon. Since they operate and keep custody of all land and village records, people have to go to them often for procuring authentic copies of those records (the most common being the 7/12 register) to get loans, subsidies and for many other purposes. *Talatis* are known to demand large bribes for *varsai* (land inheritance papers) certificates.

It is also noteworthy that groups in Meghraj and Bhiloda taluks of Sabarkantha, which has more educated and employed leaders, have been less active in issues which involve struggle and fight for social justice. They seem to be concentrating more on economic and developmental activities rather than on issues of social justice. They also seem to prefer a managerial and manipulative style to a mobilizational and agitational style. They tend to prefer the network of personal contacts, use of go-betweens, and evoking tribal affinity with government officials and lower level political leaders to get work done.

Educational, Social Reform and Awareness Activities

Twenty-one out of thirty-eight groups are quite substantially involved in educational and general information awareness activities while thirteen groups are involved in social reform activities.

Some groups have started full-fledged separate educational institutions which are discussed in the section on spin-off in the previous chapter. Some groups have started *balwadis*, non-formal and adult education classes, libraries and special coaching classes for tribal and backward class students to improve their performance in examinations. Six groups are managing *balwadis* and five groups are running adult education classes. Abhlod has started both a library and a special coaching class.

Some groups are helping to strengthen the on-going educational activities in their communities in different ways. After considerable correspondence with the government, Vantda has been successful in getting one more teacher for the local primary school. It has also donated furniture to the school and taken a subcontract to construct a school building. The Chunakhan group has done fencing and extension of the school building. Similarly Kundol has helped in repairs and renovation of the primary school building and also started a hostel for tribal youth under a Social Welfare Board scheme.

Along with formal educational work, some mandals have also undertaken vocational and cultural educational activities. Jalampur got a sewing class for their village, though its charge was given to a private person by the government. Chunakhan has given training to farmers in improved methods of agriculture. Poshina organized several *shibirs* for tribal youth on how to get information about government development programmes. Gamdi and Chunakhan groups organize sports activity, cultural programmes and *bhajan mandalis*.

Most groups felt the need for social reform activities. Some groups do it in a formal and intensive fashion, others do it as and when they find an appropriate occasion. One of the major social reform activities that the groups have undertaken is the fight against drinking. They find that drinking is one habit that has ruined the tribals. Besides their health, it ruins them financially. As soon as an adivasi gets some money he first goes to a liquor shop and spends it on drinking and perhaps even incurs a debt. He tends to lose on any major transaction that he enters into—selling or mortgaging land, negotiations about marriage, division of property—when it is done under the influence of liquor. Wife and child abuse, quarrels and fights with friends and family members, and disturbance of peace in the community are all, according to leaders of the groups, the result of widespread drinking habit among the tribals. According to the leaders, this also leads to police exploitation as the police frequently threaten arrest under the Prohibition Act whenever they want a bribe of money or even a chicken. Because of their drinking habit tribals are easy prey to the wiles of money-lenders, landlords, village brokers, compromisers and go-betweens.

Some groups continuously propogate against drinking whenever they find an opportunity. The Pangarbai mandal in Dharampur carried out an intensive struggle against a shopkeeper who used to sell black jaggery used for making liquor. He was eventually ousted from the village. Several other groups in Dharampur have prohibited drinking within the village. Kagda Mahuda group has now made the community pass a resolution that anybody who drinks will not be allowed to participate in any village gathering or attend social or religious gatherings. In Isri-Kundol the incidence of drinking among adivasis is negligible, but the Thakardas drink heavily. The group has made a special effort to educate and persuade the Thakardas to give up drinking. Gamdi village has seven distillers and sellers of liquor. The group has offered them a free buffalo if they switch over to selling milk instead of liquor. Vangad and several other groups claim that they have been very successful in either eradicating or drastically reducing the drinking habit in their villages.

One other important activity that some of the groups carry out is arbitration and mediation in internal disputes. One of the major reasons of tribal exploitation is frequent and common disputes and feuds. These occur over marriage, adultery, misbehaviour with married women, property divisions, family matters, friendships turned into enmities, old family rivalries over some injustice or murder, thefts and robberies. In the tribal belt of Poshina-Lambadia, about Rs. 2,00,000 are spent every year in the form of one village paying fines to another (colloquially called 'paying revenge') for murder—which is a common occurrence. Contributions are collected from every household belonging to the concerned tribe and all have to pay. Such fines range from Rs. 15,000 to 25,000.

When disputes occur, the matter is usually taken to the caste council (the *panch*) by one of the parties. If the matter is not resolved an official complaint is filed with the police and the matter settled in court. Often the arbitration by the traditional *panch* is unsatisfactory and unjust because they can be influenced by money or other favours. They inflict heavy punishment and fines. After the arbitration, one or both of the contenders give dinners with non-vegetarian food and alcohol. In Panchmahals, both among adivasis and Koli-Bariyas, the marriage negotiator, called *Bhanjgadio* is an institution. He keeps track of eligible boys and girls, initiates the proposal of marriage, mediates between the parties and finally settles the marriage. Sometimes he also plays the role of an arbitrator in disputes. The president of the Vangad group is a *Bhanjgadio*. The *Bhanjgadio* is a respected figure and though generally not paid is offered food and liquor. His wrath may result in the boys and girls of a particular social group or village being boycotted for marriage.

Recourse to official machinery is almost always ruinous. Repeated trips to towns, where police stations and courts are located, have to be made. On these trips the concerned party is almost always accompanied by a one or two go-betweens or a *Bhanjgadio* whose expenses including food and liquor have to be borne by the concerned party. Almost always bribes have to be paid. Small courtesies like cigarettes, tea or snacks have to be offered to the police and other petty officials. One major dispute and an adivasi goes deep into debt, not only because he spends but also because he stops earning. He ends up selling assets like land and ornaments.

Some mandals have, therefore, taken up this activity of arbitration and mediation by conducting village courts of justice. In taking up this activity the mandals' purpose is not only to save the tribals from debts, exploitation and cheating, but also to settle disputes amicably and to reduce incidence of quarrels, rivalries, feuds and murders among the community members.

In some cases as in Nagvav, Isri-Kundol, and Kundawada these activities are taken up on an informal and ad hoc basis. Whenever group leaders come to know about such problems, they intervene and persuade the parties to compromise. Some groups like Vangad and Gamdi do it formally and systematically as a group activity.

In Gamdi, usually on a Sunday, the mandal president or some other member of the executive committee holds court where parties present their cases. At times negotiations are taken up with concerned parties individually by taking them aside and then jointly. Such proceedings take between twenty minutes to six hours or repeated meetings over several weeks. In the beginning the traditional *panch* members were associated with these courts but were not allowed to play a leading role. After the court the *panch* members would often go to the houses of the concerned parties and demand liquor and food. When the group came to know about this they decided to tell the concerned parties that they should not offer any such thing to the *panch* as they had already paid the fines. The fine amount levied by the court of the mandal is small. After the dispute is settled, coconut and jaggery is bought and distributed to the people in the village instead of asking the parties to give expensive dinners with liquor. As a result of these tactics the role of the traditional *panch* became insignificant. They lost interest and now they really do not come to attend or participate. Thus without confronting them the mandal has made the *panch* dysfunctional.

During the arbitration larger interests and well-being of the parties are also kept in mind, which calls for skill, tact and wisdom. Two cases would illustrate the point. In one case there was a dispute between a husband and a wife. The wife belonged to Gamdi village while the husband belonged to another village and was working in a town in Saurashtra far from his village. The wife had left her husband's house and had come back to her parents. The husband and his brother came to the wife's parents house in Gamdi and asked for a divorce and the return of the bride price and ornaments that they had given to her at the time of marriage. When the girl's father called in Bhalabhai, the president of the mandal, the president told the husband that they should return the next Sunday with a ten rupee stamp paper as any agreement reached would have legal validity only if it was on paper bearing court stamp. Meanwhile Bhalabhai made inquiries and found that there was no major problem between the husband and the wife. Both liked each other and did not want to separate. But under the pressure and influence of the elder brother and his family, the husband had fought with his wife and was now asking her for a divorce.

The husband's brother wanted to buy some land and had asked his younger brother for money. When the younger brother said that he had no money, the elder brother asked him to sell his wife's ornaments. When the wife refused to part with them the husband felt that he was insulted and had lost face before his family. Moreover, the couple were childless. So the elder brother was insisting that the husband divorce her and get married again. Bhalabhai felt that given time, with the husband at his place of work away from the influence of his family, a reconciliation may be effected. So on the Sunday when the husband came back with his elder brother and some other relatives, Bhalabhai had several rounds of talks with them individually and jointly.

He told them that divorce cannot be given immediately as legally there has to be a three month period of separation. He also told them that in case of divorce, the bride price will not be returned as the husband's party was asking for the divorce. Moreover, the husband will have to provide alimony till such time as the woman 'does another home' (remarries). The husband's party went back. After about two months there was a village fair. It was arranged by the president that the couple meet there by themselves without the presence of the elder brother of the husband. At the fair the couple met, reconciled and left straight for the husband's workplace.

In another case, an owner of a liquor shop came to the mandal's court with a complaint that a person who had come for a drink to his shop had misbehaved with his wife. The shop owner was told that the mandal's court would take up his case on condition that he stop distilling and selling liquor, because so long as he continued with his business such incidents would occur repeatedly. He agreed.

The mandal then took up the case and asked the culprit to give Rs. 100 to the agrieved party and fined him Rs. 40. In a regular court of law the two parties would have ended up spending much more money and time.

The Gamdi mandal claims to have dealt with nearly 100 cases. while it cannot be said that arbitration work has reduced village disputes, it is certainly true that it has saved people from financial exploitation and harrassment including occasional beatings by the police.

Among other social reform work, some groups have systematically taken up activities to persuade people to change what they call *kurivaj* (bad customs). These deal with major expenses on the occasion of marriage and for performing death rituals. Incurring heavy debts on bride price, expensive caste dinners, buying ornaments, and the discomfort, disfigurement and disease which women have to suffer because of the custom of putting on heavy ornaments of silver or other metals,[5] are some of the prevalent 'bad' customs which mandals have taken up for their reform activities.

Most groups talk about this to individuals and to community members whenever opportunities like religious festivals, marriage gatherings or *bhajan mandalis* take place. The Poshina group from the most backward area of Sabarkantha district has been very active in taking up the issue of *kurivaj* and particularly the exploitation of women in tribal society.

Some groups like Chunakhan, Abhlod and Vangad are handling these issues more systematically. In the process group members have got actively involved with the caste *panch*. Since the caste group covers several villages known as *goi* (circle) or *patti* (belt) for social relations, the mandal workers have to extend their interaction beyond their villages. For instance, the Kharoda Youth Mandal (a small group in Panchmahals not funded by OXFAM and not included in this study), has formed a committee for social reform in which leaders of Abhlod and Vangad groups are also involved. In a large caste gathering organized by them several resolutions have been passed.

[5] The tribal women have to wear ornaments, sometimes weighing as much as one kilogram. These are thick, heavy and non-flexible anklets, bracelets and necklaces. Since many tribals now cannot afford to wear silver ornaments they use another cheaper, lead-like white metal called *kathir*. This metal is said to cause skin diseases.

1. At the beginning of a marriage ceremony it is customary to have liquor flow out of a hole in a pot which the people must drink by cupping their hands. It was agreed to substitute tea for alcohol in this ritual.
2. In the marriage songs called *fatana* both parties abuse each other. The meeting recommended a stop to this practice.
3. Earlier, if there was no child during the first one or two years of marriage the woman was generally divorced. It was decided to wait for seven years before divorcing the wife.
4. All Bhil women have to get their bodies tatooed. The meeting recommended a stop to this practice.
5. Women have to wear saris with *kachhoto*.[6] It was recommended that women should be allowed to wear saris without *kachhoto*.
6. The amount of bride price was reduced from Rs. 7,000 or more to Rs. 2,000.
7. Light ornaments instead of the heavy ones, and small and flexible anklets and necklaces were recommended.
8. It was also decided to call a major convention of 120 villages to further the programme of abolishing *kurivaj*.

Besides these, many groups continuously take up issues of general awareness like sending children to school, family planning, cleanliness, regular bathing and cleaning of children, use of medicines and doctors instead of quacks and faith-healers.

Implications of Social Action, Social Reform and Awareness Activities

1. Groups involved in social action activities are in general quite active and vibrant. Exceptions to this are the Jamran and Zalod groups in Panchmahals. They were active in social justice issues at one time but now seem to be disintegrating. This is so because their leaders seem to have developed other interests and are not spending much time with the mandal and its activities.
2. On the other hand, groups concentrating only on economic

---

[6] In this style of wearing the sari, the front portion from the waist down is bunched up passed between the legs and tied at the back.

activities or even developmental activities often tend to stagnate. In Sabarkantha nearly six groups out of fifteen, all of them primarily involved in economic and/or developmental activities, seem to be deteriorating or stagnating. Isri-Kundol was one of the pioneering groups and some of the leaders are still quite active in other institutions. But as their major preoccupation is developmental activities, they seem to have got more involved with other institutions that they have developed—the milk cooperative, highschool and hostel. The mandal does not seem to have remained a focal point of their activity. Although they were identified as a core group they have not been active in generating any new groups over the last two years. On the other hand, Gamdi and Abhlod in Panchmahals, in spite of having started several new institutions in which they are very involved, have kept their mandals active. In Panchmahals, four out of six groups highly active in social justice issues have remained active. Similarly, in Sabarkantha too, among the inactive and stagnant groups are mostly those which had not taken up any major social justice issues.

3. Social action tends to make the groups more inclusive and participatory. Groups in Dangs and Dharampur, Zalod and Zamran in their most active phases and Gamdi, Abhlod, Poshina and Jalampur are all much more participatory than cooperative societies. To be sure other factors like the leaders' own commitment, motivation and integrity are also factors that determine participation and involvement of members.

4. Social action activities help leaders to learn tactics, skills and strategies of mobilizing and managing movements. Both leaders and communities begin to understand the wiles of exploiters and intricacies of exploitation.

5. Contrary to what one would expect the confidence and morale of the groups have almost always gone up when they have setbacks or have to face a backlash from vested interests, as in Dangs, Mithibor and Poshina.

6. The confidence of even ordinary members and community members goes up remarkably. For the first time, people who have known only suppression and who have accepted exploitation and oppression as the norm of life realize that

they do not have to be helpless and succumb to injustice and exploitation. This is most dramatically evident in such backward communities like Mithibor in Chhotaudaipur, Pangarbari, Kosimpada, Mordanad in Dharampur, Pimpari and Sarvar in Dangs and Poshina in Khedbrahma.

7. The credibility and influence of leaders is greater, than when the groups confine themselves only to economic activities, because the interaction with members is closer and more open. The sharing is both more intimate and genuine, as they have to put up a joint front, go together to police stations, prisons and courts or rush suddenly to rescue a fellow member who is being intimidated or beaten up.

8. Like social justice activities, social reform and general awareness activities also help the group to generate greater participation and involvement of the community members.

9. Unlike economic activities, these activities are more inclusive and extensive. It does not matter whether the person to whom help is extended is a member of the group or not.

10. As to the social reform activities they need to be understood from their own perceptions and aspirations. The 'radical', 'rationalist' or 'culturist' may consider these a waste of time and energy, dysfunctional or even unfortunate because such activities are supposed to make them emulate upper, urban or modern life style and culture.

One argument against the social reform activities generally by the radical groups is that these are minor problems if at all. Why should the down-trodden people waste their time and energy criticizing their own culture and customs and thus create divisions among themselves, when the real enemy is outside, the vested interest, the establishment and an oppressive system (an argument very similar to that being put forward by Hindu revivalists at the time of the national movement).

The rationalist may argue that given their context their customs and habits are very functional. Liquor gives them more calories which they badly need, relieves their tensions and the aches and pains after a hard day's work. The father takes the bride price because he is losing an economic unit and bride price gives women equality and better status. Polygamy produces more children, and children are an economic asset for the poor. The *kachhoto* sari is convenient for doing farm work in.

The culturist may rue that social reform activities are an apeing of the urban and the modern, the loss of a richer and aesthetically superior culture. *Mahuda*[7] is very tasteful and mellow; tattoos are beautiful; the anklets, bracelets and necklaces look artistic; the *fatanas* are vigorous, uninhibited and natural.

But to workers of the groups their *kurivaj* come in the way of what they see as their progress. They see in liquor and the bride price the real reasons for the tribal's exploitation and ruin. The young men and women do not like *kachhoto*, tattoos, and the heavy ornaments. As Gopalbhai of Kharoda group put it, our young men do not like to marry girls with tattoos and *kachhoto*. And the tribal women at the Kanjetha *shibir* vehemently opposed the *fatanas*, the bride price, polygamy and liquor. They also see their reform activities as a process of liberation from the influence and control of their own traditional leaders.

11. Just as the group leaders are liquidating the political brokers by doing development activities, so are they making their old, traditional leaders redundant, some of whom themselves are political brokers or occupy important positions in panchayat and other public institutions, by doing social reform and mediation activities. Even in social matters like marriage, education of children, division of property, negotiations for house or land, advice about what to grow on their lands, the villagers are increasingly flocking to these younger group leaders. The hold of old traditional caste leaders and money-lenders in these villages has decreased perceptibly.

12. These activities have enabled the group to 'reach up and pull down' the benefits of government programmes to the weaker sections.

13. At the same time it has enabled them to 'reach out and pull in' members of their own communities. Many groups have reported increased attendance in schools and adult education classes, greater use of medical facilities, lower consumption of liquor, adoption of better agricultural methods and turning away from money-lenders and traders.

---

[7] Liquor produced from *mahuda* flowers.

7

The Groups and their World

As the groups carry on their activities, they have to relate to and interact with different sections of society. The degree and nature of interaction depend on the environment, the orientations and activities of the leaders, the strength of the groups and the perceptions of the outsiders.

So far, the world of most groups is limited to their taluk and district. Only two or three groups have developed linkages up to the state level. The major elements in their interaction are their own communities and the traditional leadership of the communities, other groups, local bureaucracy and administration, politics and other established voluntary organizations.

Groups and their Communities

Most of the thirty-eight groups that we have included in this study are now well established in their communities, and the communities have come to accept their existence. Some groups, like Tembda and Poshina, function in multicaste communities, which acquire the social characteristics of a small town. In such cases the groups' area of activity is confined to the weaker communities only to the exclusion of other social groups. For instance, though Lambadia group has formally included nearly twenty villages within its area of operation, its office holders come from villages other than Lambadia proper.

In the case of Navyuvak Pragati Mandal, though its headquarter is Poshina, its activities are really centred in the villages surrounding Poshina village. The group does not cater to social groups like Muslims, Rajputs and Banias, who live in Poshina village. Barring groups like Lambadia and Poshina all other groups are in predominantly one or two-caste villages which do not have upper castes in substantial numbers.

Some groups have faced opposition from community members who are not part of the group. Generally such conflicts or tensions are with entrenched community leaders like elders of the tribe, landlords, traders and the *sarpanch* of the village panchayat. Sometimes individuals in the community holding no particular position, but who are corrupt or bullies or have personal rivalry with group leaders, also create difficulties in the working of the groups. This is simply because the activities of the groups threaten the power, influence and domination of established leaders. Groups which have faced somewhat overt opposition are Poshina and Navavenpur in Sabarkantha, Mithibor in Chota Udepur taluk, Pangarbari and Gundia in Dharampur and to a lesser extent Gamdi, Abhlod, Lavaria and Jamran in Panchmahals.

The established sections of the community wielding power in Poshina have tried hard to obstruct the functioning of the group but it has so far stood its ground. It is one of the most well-established and cohesive groups. On the other hand, it has not been able to make any dent on the power centres of the village establishment, except that the *sarpanch*, who was once hostile, has changed his attitude and is now sympathetic.

The Mithibor group of Chota Udepur taluk, does not get along well with the panchayat *sarpanch*, who, according to the group, collaborates with the exploiters. However, the group is increasingly gaining ground in the community and the *sarpanch*, though he does not like the group, has not directly confronted them. The *sarpanch* is very close to the Vora traders who give him importance and wine and dine him frequently. The deputy *sarpanch*, who is against the *sarpanch*, is trying to keep some liaison with the group. It is also noteworthy that the taluk panchayat president has tried to create a direct rapport with the president of this group, bypassing the village *sarpanch*, because he felt that the group may influence the voting in Mithibor village.

Notably, the groups of the Isri-Kundol area and Chunakhan in Sabarkantha have not faced any great opposition from community leaders. This is perhaps because, as we have earlier mentioned, the adivasis of Meghraj and Bhiloda are more advanced. The group leaders themselves are relatively educated, economically better off and many of them are in government service and so it is somewhat difficult to oppose them. Because Poshina, Mithibor, Jamran and the villages of Dharampur area are backward, the domination of entrenched interests is high. They feel more directly threatened but also feel bold enough to put up a resistance, at least initially.

The opposition resorts to threatening group leaders, as in Poshina, and shouting and trying to disrupt meetings or questioning the legality of the loan distribution activity—'Who has given them the authority to do this work?'—as in Navavenpur or Abhlod. Sometimes they contact government officials and tell them not to help the mandal, as in the case of Panganbari when community leaders opposing the group asked the *mamlatdar* not to recognize the mandal's shop as a fair-price ration shop; or to institute an inquiry, as in Gamdi and Zalod. Most often, they instigate community members against mandal leaders with misleading statements like 'Why don't they give more loans?' 'Why have they not given loans to everybody?'—they have got a lot of money.' 'Why do they charge five per cent more on loans when OXFAM does not charge any interest?' and spreading rumours questioning the honesty and integrity of mandal leaders, as in Gamdi, Poshina, Abhlod and Navavenpur.

Sometimes they also try to tempt and corrupt mandal leaders as in Mithibor, Poshina or Abhlod, and in rare cases they try to physically harm the leaders as happened in Gamdi, when the incumbent *sarpanch* lost the election against the mandal's candidate and started a drunken brawl.

In most cases, however, they have not been successful in harming the mandals to any great extent. The mandals have withstood such onslaughts very well because their activities have shown results, or because mandals have established themselves so well that attempts to harm them have not been successful. The mandals have, with time, acquired considerable influence in their communities. The power weilders in the village panchayats, for instance, are either part of the groups or have been overpowered by the groups. Further, some groups like Gamdi and Abhlod have captured village panchayats, whereas Pangarbari village in Dharampur tried but was not successful as an established Christian Mission supported their rival. Groups which have acquired considerable influence in their communities are: Lavaria, Gamdi, Margala, Abhlod and Vangad in Panchmahals and Isri-Kundol, Kagda Mahuda, Jalampur, Vantda and Chunakhan in Sabarkantha. Dharampur groups are as yet too new to have any major impact but they do have substantial support from their communities.

Nevertheless, conflict with established community leaders has sometimes made mandal leaders anxious and worried. In some cases, it has cramped their activities. For instance, the Navavenpur president said that he does not dare charge five per cent more on loans, to raise the mandal's funds, because he is worried that the community will question his integrity. He also shies away from calling general meetings. Abhlod mandal, in spite of its many activities and high degree of success, has taken a soft stand on collecting membership dues and recovery of loans. Pangarbari leaders were thinking of closing down the fair price ration shop because of criticism and allegations by the rival group in the community.

On the other hand such opposition has brought the leaders closer to the people. They have to explain their side of the matter; and on the whole such opposition has also pushed them to share their problems with ordinary members.

Relationship among Groups

We have discussed earlier the role of core groups which has been one of the modes of intergroup help and support. But it has been limited to mobilizing people for forming groups and initial guidance and support. Such interaction reduced considerably once the groups were set up.

Another mode of interaction is one in which groups from adjoining areas interact. This has been possible because such groups are near each other and leaders know each other well, have opportunities to meet at bus stops, in taluk towns, or at religious or social gatherings. Several such spontaneous interacting clusters of groups can be identified. Such clusters of groups are listed below:

1. Isri-Kundol area: Isri-Kundol, Mota Kantharia, Kagda Mahuda, Jalampur, Vantda, Chhitadara, Isri-Kundol Women's group.
2. Khedbrahma area: Poshina, Tembda, Lambadia.
3. Zalod area: Zalod, Vangad, Margala, Gamdi.

4. Devgadh Baria area: Mithibor, Jamran, Lavaria, Nagvav, Kundawada, Satkunda.
5. Dharampur area: All the groups.

In Sabarkantha district, Chunakhan, Navavenpur, Gambhoi Bamboo Cooperative, Vantda Vatrak Bamboo Cooperative and Vantda Milk Cooperative seem to be the most isolated groups. They do not appear to have much interaction with any other group.

In interaction of this type, the groups may compare notes, give information to each other about some new activity or programme, and sometimes guide or advice. But such interaction is usually not frequent and intensive. In Dharampur the newly established groups have tried to study and understand the activities of other groups and patterned their organization and their activities accordingly. Their interaction and mutual help is also more frequent. The third mode of interaction is the *shibirs* which we have already discussed in detail earlier.

The fourth, and potentially the most important mode, is the new structure of the district-level union or association of groups, which is being developed both in Sabarkantha and Panchmahals. During the Isri-Kundol *shibir* the participants had also held meetings in small groups and decided to form a kind of federation of small groups at the district level. Two ad hoc committees, one each for Panchmahals and Sabarkantha district, were formed.

Panchmahals has already moved ahead and registered the union. In Sabarkantha the ad hoc committee could not become active in this matter. However, in the *shibir* held at Madha (Dungarpur district, Rajasthan) in July 1984, the Sabarkantha groups got inspired by the Panchmahals example and decided to join the Sabar Yuva Vikas Mandal, which is an existing group with district-wide area of operation. This mandal has agreed to be converted into an association of mandals and will make necessary changes in its constitution.

The Panchmahals union of groups, called Panchmahal Zilla Adivasi Yuvak Mandal Sangh, completes nearly two years of registration. It has thirty-five registered small groups (including some which are not supported by OXFAM as yet) as members. The group has met several times. At present it has not started many substantive activities[1] with regard to groups. As yet it is involved with its own organizational matters. It has decided to establish three offices in different parts of the district which will be used for groups of the neighbouring areas. The group has designated one of the executive committee members to help other groups with accounts and book-keeping.

It is visualized that the district-level union would arrange training programmes, help other groups if they face major problems of injustice or suppression, arrange for legal aid, and help individual groups to follow up and pursue problems at the district and state levels. But all this depends on how this district-level association shapes up. The association may turn into a platform for some group leaders to create their own constituencies. If they are politically ambitious they may use the association for their personal political gains. There were already signs of a power struggle in the Panchmahals association during its election meeting held in July 1984. Some ambitious leaders had canvassed for support, and in order to gain the support evoked a technicality that they could not hold elections till two years of registration were complete. Some adjustments were made in the executive committee to satisfy the dissidents.

All interactions among groups is so far confined to group leaders who form the executive committee of the union. It has not reached the level of interaction between ordinary members of different groups. This can be generated by intergroup visits and by holding *shibirs* primarily for members rather than leaders.

Small Groups and Administration

Discussion on activities of the groups has already dealt with patterns of interaction with administration. Since most development is financed, controlled and administered by the government they have to interact very intensively with government administration. There are two major patterns in this interaction. One is of confrontation and assertion of their rights; insistance that the bureau-

---

[1] According to the latest report it had organized a training camp for women in the monsoon of 1984. From informal information gathered, it appears that the district association in Panchmahals has taken up many activities including famine relief work during the years 1985 and 1986.

cracy must serve them. The other is of manipulation through parochial or political linkages.

Groups which have educated leaders in government service take recourse to the latter option more often. The groups of Isri-Kundol area, Chunakhan in Sabarkantha, and Gamdi, Abhlod and Vangad in Panchmahals generally follow this pattern.

Groups like Mithibor, Jamran and Lavaria in Panchmahals, and Poshina in Sabarkantha and all groups in Dharampur take recourse to the more direct approach of confrontation and assertion of their rights.

Though Gamdi, Abhlod and Vangad had to resolve some issues through direct confrontation and satyagraha as we have already seen for most of their work they take recourse to manipulative tactics. Groups like Chunakhan, Isri-Kundol, Mota Kantharia, Gamdi, Abhlod and Zalod have office bearers and executive committee members who are working in the government. Moreover, they have a few other people from their villages in government service. They have political linkages, too. Thus, parochial ties of tribe, friendship and villages are invoked to make the administration respond. As a result, these groups are also able to play the role of go-betweens and facilitators more successfully.

The local administration, generally, does not like the group phenomenon, as now they have to cope with one more pressure, more determined and more organized. For the corrupt, incompetent, or irregular government functionaries the groups pose a great problem. Sometimes they try to harass the groups by delaying, making them run around, raising technicalities and not readily facilitating their work by raising objections like 'application forms are out of stock', 'the date for application is over', 'all the necessary information is not supplied', 'certificates of talati not attached'. Departments with a tradition of coercion such as those of police and forest even use physical force as we have already seen. Sometimes, attempts are made to keep leaders in line by maligning them by instituting inquiries of corruption, as in the case of Zalod and Gamdi. But generally, the bureaucracy has retreated in the face of confrontation by the groups. They stop practising corruption in villages which are covered by the groups.

Several groups have now made considerable impression on the local administration right up to the district level. We find that eight of the groups have made their mark. It is not that the other thirty groups have nothing to do with the administration. As we have already discussed earlier, groups like Jamran, Mithibor and Lavaria have carried out their fight against the administration quite successfully. We only wish to emphasize that eight groups have continuous interaction and greater response from the administration. The administration has begun to recognise them and, perhaps, be afraid of them as strong groups to be taken cognizance of. As the Abhlod president put it, 'They have now "known" us well.' The administration would now find it difficult to ignore them and for most normal work would not create obstacles nor would these groups have to fight for every work they take to the administration.

Groups and Politics[2]

Since bureaucrats rather than politicians are in the foreground, during most confrontations and fights for justice, the groups have dealt mainly with the bureaucracy. Rarely have they confronted politicians. But it does not mean that the groups had no dealings with politics, politicians or parties.

There are three major patterns of interaction: (*a*) group leaders themselves have become politicians or occupied positions in political institutions; (*b*) groups or some leaders of groups have developed political linkages, generally with individual politicians; and (*c*) groups keep a distance from politics or politicians.

We found that five of the groups have strong political linkages; six groups have some political linkages; while twenty-three groups have little or no political interaction. Most of the cooperative societies except the Tembda Cooperative have no political linkages. It is also noteworthy that among the most politicized groups, four out of nine are from Panchmahals. In Panchmahals, only two out of the nine groups for which information could be obtained were politically inactive. While in Sabarkantha nine out of thirteen groups about which information could be gathered were politically inactive. In Dharampur none of the twelve groups had any strong political linkages.

[2] Some may regard anything and everything that these groups do as political or having political implications. My reference here is to elections, parties, politicians and positions in political institutions.

It is important to understand the mechanism of these linkages. Given below are some examples:

The brother-in-law of the president of Isri-Kundol was a member of the state executive of the Congress-I and President of the District Congress-I party. The president himself supported the Janata Party. The Ashramshala of which he was the principal was sponsored and managed by a Gandhian voluntary agency whose workers were said to support the Janata Party. During the 1980 elections he and other office bearers of the group had canvassed for the the Janata Party.

The president of the Tembda Cooperative was an ex-member of the Legislative Assembly to which he was elected as a Swatantra Party member.

The president of the Chunakhan group was in close touch with the MLA of the constituency. According to him all group members and the village were Congress-I supporters. The group may in the coming elections put up a candidate, though not officially, as the group's candidate.

The father of the president of the Abhlod Yuvak Mandal was a Congress-I member in the district panchayat. The group had close connections with a Deputy Minister at the state level, and got many of its problems solved through this connection.

The president of the Zalod group was a member of the Zalod town panchayat. He had contested the Legislative Assembly election twice—once from the Jansangh and once from the Congress (Urs) Party.

The Vangad group had an executive committee member who was a Janata Party member of the district panchayat, and another one who was a Congress-I member in the taluk panchayat.

The Gamdi mandal very actively participated in panchayat elections and its involvement in politics was quite complicated. In the taluk panchayat elections, a middle-aged person was contesting from the Congress-I party in Gamdi constituency. The group leaders decided that they should have a younger person. One of the executive committee members was put up as a candidate from the Janata Party. The group leaders canvassed vigorously from house to house and got their Janata Party candidate elected.

In the district panchayat elections, the same Gamdi group had asked one of its executive committee members to contest the elections. However, his father's friend was contesting and so he was pressurised to withdraw. The group supported his father's friend, who was a Congress-I candidate. The group canvassed for him actively and got him elected. However, the Congress-I party did not give him any position as president, vice-president or chairman of a committee in the district panchayat for which he was striving. Since the Congress-I had a majority of only one, he crossed over to the Janata Party. The Gamdi mandal did not approve of it because they felt that their candidate should have asked them before crossing over. Moreover, the Gamdi group had organized a satyagraha against the irregularity of the state transport bus and had asked him to remain present and support the satyagraha which he did not. So they decided to get rid of him.

In the mid-term elections to the zilla panchayat they made efforts to get a Congress-I nomination for the same candidate whom they had earlier defeated in the taluk panchayat elections, by putting up their own executive committee member as a Janata Party candidate. They got him the Congress-I nomination and got him elected against the same person whom they had earlier got elected!

According to the president of the Gamdi group, the executive committee members get together to decide their course of action in the elections and then vigorously campaign for the person they decide to support. So far they have always been successful. The Gamdi president said that they do not give importance to any party. They select or support a person who they believe would do 'our work.' Then they try to get him a ticket from any party which is willing to do so. The president is confident that if a person so elected betrays them (i.e., 'does not do our work'), then they could get him defeated and another one elected. He further said that in the next general elections they may put up a candidate for the State Assembly because the present MLA is not paying much attention to their constituency and to the work of the adivasis.

The groups do not undertake any political activities officially under the banner of the group.[3] No general meetings are called.

[3] Except in one case when a major rally was held in Panchmahals in March 1984, to voice the grievances of the tribals. In the leaflet printed for the purpose, an appeal was made to all tribals to attend irrespective of their party affiliation. The

No resolutions are passed or recorded. In their activity reports, they are not mentioned as activities. The decisions about political activities are taken by a few office bearers. Those groups which are more involved in political activities try to keep their personal political work and group activities separate, or at least argue that they are separate. However, in the perception of the people and politicians they are not separate and when the leaders informally talk of political activities they themselves also talk as if these were their mandal's activities.

While most groups are not loyal to any particular party (though in a given situation they may prefer to be generally supportive of a particular political party), their politics is not non-partisan.

All groups and their leaders are highly critical of 'politics' and 'politicians.' They have utter contempt for politicians whom they consider selfish, power-crazy and corrupt people. They have no regard for or faith in any political party either. Yet they do relate to existing parties and politicians. When they become politicians, they do so by joining parties, contesting elections and occupying positions in political institutions. Their styles, modus operandi and political behaviour are not markedly different from the politicians whom they despise.

Some of them are politically ambitious, and obviously they would capitalize on the strength they have acquired through their work for groups to get political mileage out of it. How that would affect the groups depend on how they try to use the groups.

But the chances are that the group leaders' politics would weaken the groups rather than strengthen them because the modus operandi that the leaders would be forced to adopt is not likely to be any different from the modus operandi of politicians in general. Since this mode of work involves compromise, manipulation, favouritism, factionalism, and even bribes and corruption, it is bound to affect the ethos of the group and consequently its functioning.

Politically ambitious, active or involved leaders of the mandals have so far not related to their members or to their communities in any political terms other than electoral. All their socially moti-

---

leaflet had the name of the secretary of the Rashtriya Congress as publisher, and had the signatures of nine of the groups' leaders, five of them signing as office bearers of their groups. In the meeting the banners and flags of the party were prominently displayed.

vated movements have been against bad, corrupt and unjust administration and administrators but not explicitly and directly against politics and politicians or against the political system or its processes.

As for the politicians, they have been watching the groups wherever they have become visible. As yet, there has not been a major occasion or necessity for them to directly involve the groups in politics. During the 1980 general elections only a small number of these groups existed and at that time they had not become very visible.

Some politicians have wondered what this phenomenon of mandals is all about. In one case it was reported that an MLA had made inquiries about the groups' source of funding, and whether they were legitimate registered groups. Whenever groups' leaders go to politicians for some work they tell the leaders that since they are doing favours for the groups, in return the groups should support them when the time (elections) comes.

Since general elections were expected to be held soon, parties and politicians had become somewhat more alert about these groups. The Rashtriya Congress had already established communication with some of the groups in Panchmahals. Besides the rally for voicing tribals' grievances that the party and the groups jointly organized in March 1984, the party kept in touch with some of these leaders. It took a major lead in organizing the tribal convention in July 1984, where leaders of the groups were invited. In fact, the invitation also carried a letter of good wishes to the convention from another activist. This activist was the president designate of the proposed state level federation of groups. The groups knew him well and he was respected by them. By enclosing his letter of good wishes for the convention, the party was trying to gain credibility with the groups. It was reported that leaders of several groups in Panchmahals attended this convention.[4] It seems inevitable that leaders of more successful and stronger groups would become politically active. And the only type of politics that they know, understand and are interested in, is partisan and electoral politics.

[4] It was reported that some group leaders from Panchmahals, notably Abhlod, Gamdi and Zalod tried to get assembly tickets during the last assembly elections. In the last Panchayat elections, in 1986, Bhalabhai of Gamdi Mandal contested the district panchayat election but was defeated.

Groups and Voluntary Agencies

There are mainly two types of established voluntary agencies in the areas where these groups have been formed: the Gandhian-sarvodaya type agencies and missionary agencies. In Panchmahals, Sadguru Seva Trust, a voluntary agency established by an industrial house is also active. These are larger, established voluntary agencies generally manned and managed by upper caste, middle and upper class well-educated people.

The Gandhian-sarvodaya agencies and the missionary agencies are very old and established agencies. They have been there for at least twenty years or more. The Bhil Seva Mandal at Dahod, for instance, is nearly sixty years old. These agencies are involved in educational and other developmental activities. They rarely get involved in mobilizational and conflict oriented struggles or movements. The Gandhian-sarvodaya agencies depend heavily on government patronage and support.

Sadguru Seva Trust is primarily involved in economic activities in Panchmahals, particularly irrigation. More recently, they have also taken up health activities.

Generally, there have not been strong links and intensive interaction between large established voluntary agencies and small groups. It seems that the large agencies are somewhat uneasy and uncomfortable with the growth of small action groups, and in two or three cases there have been direct confrontation between the two.

In Dharampur, the principal of the Pindwal Ashramshala has been taking active interest in these groups. OXFAM has identified several groups with his help. He has been playing the role of a core person. His involvement, though, is personal rather than institutional. He is not involved with the small groups on behalf of his agency—the Dakshin Gujarat Pachhat Varg Kelvani Mandal. However, in that area, there is another voluntary agency working in the same villages as the groups. While they have so far not done anything against these groups, neither have they tried to get to know the groups and barely know one or two leaders.

In Dangs, it seems that the missionary establishment does not like the Gram Vikas Mandalis. They have been supporting the entrenched and established political leaders against whom the groups are fighting. There have been reports about groups in the area being harassed and obstructed by workers of this establishment. Reportedly, the missionary establishment also tried to influence the district administration against these groups. Attempts to entice and co-opt some workers of the groups were also reported to us.

In Panchmahals, one of the groups had to threaten satyagraha when the lift irrigation scheme of one of the voluntary agencies in a nearby village resulted in the lands of the mandal's village being submerged, without the village people getting any benefit from the irrigation scheme. The agency, however, responded by starting a lift irrigation scheme at that village also. Reportedly, however, they tried to see to it that the group had no say or influence in the newly-formed irrigation society in the village.

The president of the group contested the election for the president of the irrigation society; but an attempt was made to defeat him by holding the election on a day when the president was not in the village. He was, however, elected in absentia. The agency also gave twenty pumpsets to the village independently of the group, while the group itself was also renting out a machine of its own. Consequently, the group had to take its machine to other villages.

Another group came in direct confrontation with the Ashramshala authorities managed by an established voluntary agency in the district. Finally, the group started a parallel school sponsored by the Khetvikas Parishad.

The Vangad group also fought against the TRYSEM[5] centre run by another large voluntary agency when they found that the agency was not marking attendance and paying a regular stipend. The Vangad group also alleged that the agency's workers had misappropriated money in the construction of the water hand pump.

Mithibor, which is in Baroda district, is also within the effective area of a well-established and politically powerful agency working among tribals. The Mithibor group is being watched and information is acquired about the activities of the group through the agency's contacts in the area. There has been no direct confrontation, but the powerful leader of this big and well-established agency is reportedly very uneasy about the establishment of this group, and if the Mithibor group comes into contact with or takes up an activity in which the agency has an interest, the Mithibor group will have to either fall in line or face stiff opposition.

In Sabarkantha, there are three voluntary agencies of the

---

[5] It is a government-sponsored programme for the training of rural youth.

Gandhian type and a Christian Mission working in the same areas
where some of the groups are working. Though initially OXFAM
made contact with some of the group leaders through these agencies, the agencies were not quite happy and comfortable with the
activities of these groups. Sometimes they have given the groups
some help like in the Ambar Charka scheme but generally they are
not very helpful. If the group leaders go to them for help they
taunt them, snub them or ask them to go to OXFAM. A group in
Khedbrahma badly needed some money for their work for a
temporary period of six months or so. They went to a voluntary
agency. They were given Rs. 7,000 only after they gave their
personal ornaments as collateral. The group had to pay Rs. 700
towards interest for six months at the rate of 20 per cent.

In the Isri-Kundol area, the president of one of the groups is
closely connected with a sarvodaya voluntary agency. In fact, he
was introduced to OXFAM by the agency. And yet the relationship between the group and the agency is far from positive. He
usually avoided informing the agency about his group's activities,
the amount of funds received from OXFAM or even visits by the
OXFAM field officer.

The Christian mission in Sabarkantha seems to be quite uneasy
with the groups and keeps a polite distance from them; and to
outsiders is sometimes even critical of the groups.

We held in-depth discussions with several voluntary agencies in
these districts. Although they have been working in these areas for
two decades or more, we found that they did not have much
detailed and correct information about the groups or their leaders.
Moreover, while they have worked among the adivasis for decades
they do not seem to have established either their own credibility or
mutual trust and understanding. We found a lack of information
about the groups and a complete lack of understanding about the
larger dimensions of the small group phenomenon. They also
harboured a deep cynicism about rural illiterate adivasis being able
to manage their own affairs. Many that we talked to said that the
adivasis cannot handle their problems, they cannot manage money,
they cannot be given responsibility and resources. OXFAM money
and the importance OXFAM gives them will spoil them. 'I know
OXFAM. But who is Mistry? I have never met him, he never
comes here (to his establishment). All the money spent by

OXFAM is going down the drain,' said the head of a missionary establishment. 'If the money is given to us,' emphasized the head of a Gandhian agency, 'then it will be well utilized because we know the real nature of the people here.'

In general, the established larger voluntary agencies working in the areas where mandals have been formed are either uninformed and apathetic or are quite uncomfortable and jittery with this new phenomenon of small groups of weaker sections in their areas. There are several reasons for this attitude:

1. Many of the large established agencies of the Gandhian-sarvodaya type and the missionary organizations are getting into a rut. They have become, at best, service-delivery agencies, and even here their activities and the mode of doing these are routinized. They seem to be plodding and lack dynamism and creativity. Any group, therefore, which is vibrant and active in their area is likely to make them anxious and defensive. Also, by now, most of these agencies are beginning to realize that service-delivery and welfare type of activities are not very useful. Because of this they have failed to attract young people from outside or from within the communities to their organizations. They are not able to bring themselves to undertake mobilizational, organizational and struggle activities.

2. The groups are doing much better work than some of these established agencies. The record of recovery of loans by these agencies is very poor as compared to the groups. The agencies are rarely successful in generating the participation of the poor people. If they generate participation it is mainly symbolic and at best activity-specific. (Some of them proudly brought before us one or two adivasis whom they had 'prepared'.) Again, their own approach, at its best, is not essentially different from that of the government's where the resource controlling authorities or agencies are conceptualized as the 'planning-locating-allocating-managing system' while the weak and the poor are seen as the 'receiving' system.

3. As far as missionaries are concerned their work of 'christian-

izing,' if not converting, would run into rough weather with the rise of the small groups.[6]

4. Somewhere along the way the established voluntary agencies seem to have lost sight of their mission. The agency or the institution becomes an end in itself. After all these years they are still greedily looking for money or resources from outside to increase their activities. The territorial·imperative[7] and desire to control any voluntary effort in·'our area' becomes strong. In the initial stages of OXFAM's efforts towards the development of small groups, some agencies in Sabarkantha had wanted and hoped that these efforts would be channeled through them, funds would be given to them and that they would form, patronize or manage the groups.

On the whole the world outside their own community, be it politics, government or older well established agencies with whom the groups must deal, is not very supportive. At the same time it is not as rough and hostile as one would find in some other parts of the country. So far, however, these groups have acquitted themselves creditably. They have shown amazing acumen and strength in dealing with well entrenched and resourceful individuals and organizations from the world of politics, administration and voluntary work.

---

[6] Though it needs to be mentioned that, if anything, the groups would try to bring about greater acceptance of Christian adivasis. In Meghraj and Bhiloda Taluks of Sabarkantha there is considerable Hinduization of adivasis because of the strong 'Bhagat' movement. As a result, sometimes, Christian adivasis are not treated well or social interaction with them is much less. At least one group in Sabarkantha reported making conscious efforts to tell their people not to boycott Christian adivasis and treat all adivasis as 'our brothers.'

[7] In Dharampur as in Chhota Udepur and Panchmahals we were told stories about how the established voluntary agencies would dispute the territorial boundaries of their work and how they would arrive at a 'truce' about the territorial boundaries among them indicating that the 'territorial imperative' syndrome seems to have overtaken even voluntary work.

8

The Gamdi Mandal

The Gamdi Vibhag Yuvak Mandal was started at the beginning of 1980. It is located in Gamdi village of Zalod taluk of Panchmahals district. It draws its membership from eight surrounding villages, covering approximately 1,275 households and a population of about 8,000. It is a predominantly tribal area where adivasis form more than 90 per cent of the population.

Genesis

The present president, Bhalabhai, an adivasi, has since his early youth been involved in public activities. He was a government employee working as a vaccinator in the health department when he was posted in Kanjetha village in 1972 where he founded a youth organization. Later on, he and a few other friends formed the Panchmahals Zilla Adivasi Yuvak Mandal at Zalod of which he was an active executive member till 1982. In 1979, he was transferred to Abhlod, a village in Dahod taluk of Panchmahals district. There he activated a dormant youth organization and also helped it to get ʻOXFAM funds. The Panchmahals Zilla Adivasi Yuvak Mandal of which he was an executive member had received OXFAM help. Bhalabhai knew Mistry, the OXFAM Field Officer, through this mandal. When he decided to start a mandal in his own village of Gamdi, he hoped to get OXFAM support.

He first discussed this matter with a few young people of his village who were enthusiastic about doing community work. Afterwards, a formal meeting of all villagers was called. Nearly 200 people besides many children and some women were present. The idea of starting a mandal and its format were explained. The villagers supported the idea and a membership fee of Rs. 5 per member was collected and the mandal was registered with the Charity Commissioner in January 1980.

It was decided to conduct a survey of the village to ascertain needs and problems and to decide on a plan of action. Bhalabhai as a vaccinator had carried out some surveys and knew the techniques involved. According to him, a very systematic survey was carried out and it revealed many things about the village which were new even to them.

The survey revealed that there was considerable migration from the village. Lack of irrigation resulted in only one monsoon crop. After that people migrated for work. Nearly 60 per cent of the families were either entirely or partially migrants. The survey showed that out of 450 households, only seventy-eight were somewhat well-to-do with an annual income between Rs. 7,000 to Rs. 10,000. These families had at least one member employed full-time and permanently. Twenty per cent of the households were very poor and had difficulty getting food all through the year. The survey also showed that ninety-five farmers had mortgaged 101 acres of land. Twenty five per cent of this mortgaged land were with two rich farmers of the village.

The survey findings were discussed in the general meeting. It was decided that the mandal should (*a*) approach OXFAM for funds to get the mortgaged land released; (*b*) write to IRDP for an irrigation scheme; (*c*) form cooperative societies to start some economic activity; (*d*) make attempts to get benefits of various development programmes; (*e*) write to the electricity board to electrify the village and if necessary approach higher authorities.

Membership and Leadership

As mentioned earlier the area of activity of the mandal covers eight villages. All eight villages have members in the mandal. However, the mandal draws its highest membership from village Gamdi which is also the main centre of its activities. The mandal has 213 ordinary members. The membership fee is Rs. 5 per member payable once in two years when the mandal elects its executive committee members and office bearers.

Till March 1984, the membership fees had been collected only once. The second round of collection was due in April 1983, when the election of the new executive committee was due. However, neither was the election held nor the membership fees collected.

The office bearers with whom we discussed the matter said that people are very reluctant to give any money on their own, because they are used to receiving free benefits from governmental programmes. There is also considerable apprehension that the money will be misappropriated, since people have had such experiences in the past. In matters of money there is generally a high level of distrust. The mandal has also started a few other organizations in the last two years notably two cooperatives, so nearly every six months the same people pay membership fees for some organization or the other and they are unable to understand why membership is collected so often from them.

Other than this, the community's involvement in the mandal seems quite high. Both formal and informal meetings are held frequently. The members have supported the mandal leaders on many occasions in their struggle against a corrupt and callous bureaucracy. Since the mandal is involved in running several other organizations, and since it has also organized many other village activities like sports, *bhajan mandalis*, festivals, village courts to decide disputes out of court etc., the leaders of the mandal interact with ordinary members and other villagers almost every day. Thus, there is a close interaction between community members and leaders of the mandal.

The mandal has eleven executive committee members. The background and details are given in Table 10.

As is evident from the information given in Table 10 the youngest member is 26 years old while the oldest is 42 years. This is one of the few mandals where more executive committee members are educated and hold jobs in government. Only four of the eleven executive members are dependent on agriculture though all members have some land. The landholding as reported by them is below five acres for all executive members and ten of the eleven members have reported owning land below three acres. All executive committee members are adivasis.

More members in this group, as compared to other groups that we studied, occupy some position in other institutions. But it is noteworthy that all other positions held by executive committee members, except that of police patel, have been occupied after the mandal was formed and with the conscious decision and active support of the mandal. Thus membership in taluk panchayat, chairmanship of the poultry and irrigation cooperative society were acquired with the conscious planning and organized efforts of the mandal. As we shall see later, the involvement of mandal members in local government institutions, village, taluk and district panchayats were due to active and organized efforts of the mandal.

TABLE 10
*Background Information on Executive
Committee Members of Gamdi Mandal*

Position	Age	Education	Occupation	Other Information
President	33	Two years of college	Vaccinator	Secretary Association of District Members, President of the Irrigation Society
Vice-President	34	Graduate	Teacher	—
Secretary	38	Graduate	Teacher	Member of Taluk Panchayat, Janata Party
Jt. Secretary	36	Primary School (7th Grade)	Teacher	President, Taluk Primary School Teachers' Association
Treasurer	37	Middle School (9th Grade)	Farmer	Dy. *Sarpanch* of Gamdi Village
Member	26	High School	Farmer	—
Member	30	Graduate and Law Graduate	Advocate	Member of Taluk Panchayat from Congress (I) Party
Member	34	10th Grade	Farmer	Police Patel of the Village
Member	38	10th Grade	Farmer	Secretary of the Cooperative Society
Member	28	SSC	Helper in State Transport	—
Member	42	Primary School (6th Grade)	Village Postmaster	Chairman of the Poultry Cooperative Society of Gamdi Village

An unusual feature of this mandal is that each executive committee member contributes to the mandal's work based on his special capability, skill or position. For instance, the vicepresident has a motorcycle and, therefore, he is involved in contacting people in the surrounding villages, in carrying messages and in mobilizing support. During taluk panchayat elections and at the time of the satyagraha that the mandal carried out against the State Transport Corporation he undertook the major work of going round and convincing people to participate. The treasurer does all routine work in connection with government offices. Another member who is a lawyer helps people who are involved in revenue and police cases. He sees to it that revenue and police officials do not cheat, exploit or harass the people. He does not charge fees for fighting the cases of mandal members. The executive member who works as a helper in the State Transport can travel in the public bus without having to pay the fare. So he generally takes up work related to the mandal and its members which requires going to the taluk and district headquarter offices. Another executive member, who is a secretary of the cooperative society, knows a lot about cooperative activity, its laws and procedures. He guides people so that they can benefit from the cooperative activities. He has very good contacts with people so he knows who among the local bureaucrats, politicians, businessmen and traders or other village elites exploit people. People confide in him about such incidents of exploitation. He brings such incidents to the mandal's notice and helps the mandal in fighting against petty corruption and exploitation. Another member is a trader. He is known to be a good and honest businessman in the area and has close contacts with his customers. He actively participates in the mandal's activities, accompanies other mandal leaders to the government offices located at taluk headquarters and also provides many useful contacts.

Funding

The mandal's main source of support has been OXFAM. So far, between 1980 and 1982, OXFAM has given Rs. 62,500 for various activities as follows:

Amount (Rs.)	Date of Disbursement	Purpose
1,500	29.10.1980	Training tour of some members
10,000	04.10.1981	For buying diesel pumps for irrigation
1,000	25.06.1981	Administrative expenses
20,000	19.10.1981	For giving loans to members for buying bullocks
10,000	19.10.1982	For releasing mortgaged land
20,000	30.10.1982	For releasing mortgaged land

Over and above this the mandal has been able to develop a small fund of its own. The mandal hires out a diesel pump for irrigation and earns a very small profit: in the first year the profit earned was only Rs. 250. It also charges five per cent commission on the money it loans to its members. The commission is deducted at the time of giving loans. Such funds help the mandal to take care of its administrative expenses such as stationery, fee for auditors, travel expenses etc. On the whole, however, the mandal has not been able to generate any sizable fund on its own to carry out its activities without external financial help. Nor are there any signs that it will be able to do so in the future. According to the president, people are very reluctant to give any money to the mandal, even their membership fees. Very few people willingly and regularly pay their membership fees or make any other contribution. Even when they do, they give initially, to start the activities (e.g., forming a cooperative society), but once the activities start they are reluctant to give money on a regular basis.

The diesel pump which OXFAM had originally funded to enable the mandal to generate its own funds has not worked out well. After meeting the cost of the bullock and the bullock cart for transferring the diesel pump from place to place and the salary of the man to look after the running of the pump, water distribution, maintenance and repairs of the pump, very little profit was left. In the first year, the mandal earned a net profit of Rs. 250 only. As it had to return Rs. 2,000 to OXFAM towards the annual instalment against the loan of Rs. 10,000, it found it impossible even to continue with this activity. Ultimately they requested OXFAM to convert the loan into a grant after paying the first instalment of Rs. 2,000.

So far, in its three years of functioning, the mandal has very little by way of its own funds. However, at the moment, it has enough funds from OXFAM to continue its activities.

The funds that OXFAM has given are all in the nature of revolving funds, except Rs. 1,500 for training and Rs. 1,000 for administrative expenses which were outright grants, besides the Rs. 10,000 for the diesel pump subsequently converted into a grant.

OXFAM has given money in instalments because it wanted to first see how the money was being expended. They gave more money as they saw the proper management of funds by the mandal and as the need arose.

Since 1982, OXFAM has not given any money to the mandal. According to OXFAM, now the mandal will have to manage its own affairs with the money given so far and generate other sources of income if necessary.

Economic Activities

The major economic activity that the mandal undertook was giving loans to those members who had mortgaged their lands. As discussed earlier the mandal in its bench-mark survey had found that many farmers who had mortgaged their land were very poor. They did not even have enough food throughout the year. So the mandal decided to concentrate on this activity. In 1982 it distributed loans for which OXFAM had given Rs. 30,000. Fifty-six farmers from four villages including Gamdi village were given Rs. 31,350. The additional amount of Rs. 1,350, which the mandal had earned from charging a five per cent service charge on earlier loans, was also utilized. Ninety-six acres of land was thus released. The mandal could recover Rs. 3,465 from the first round of loans which was lent again to three new farmers.

In giving loans the mandal's criterion was not to give the full amount needed. The loanee farmers had to contribute also. Thus most farmers were given loans between Rs. 400 to 700; except in the case of one farmer who was very poor and, therefore, was given the full amount of Rs. 1,200. The mandal workers did not stop at merely giving loans, but followed up by witnessing the actual transaction whereby the mortgaged land was released, to ensure that the loanees got back their land and did not get cheated. The workers also actively followed up with the farmers who got back their lands to see that they cultivated them.

This particular activity, according to mandal workers, has greatly helped very poor farmers. Eighteen farmers have completely stopped going out of the village in search of work, while some others do so for a fewer number of days. Only three of the fifty-six farmers have remortgaged their lands. One farmer had to remortgage his land because he was afflicted by paralysis, and needed money for his livelihood. Another needed money for the treatment of his wife who was seriously ill. The third remortgaged his land to pay dowry for his son's marriage. Loan recovery is not very good. The reasons are: people are reluctant to return loans because they are accustomed to receiving free help from public institutions. They have learnt from their own and others' experiences that nothing much happens if they do not repay governmental and institutional debts. Secondly, they are so poor that they have very little surplus left. If at all there is any surplus they spend it on their social and religious obligations. Social and religious obligations such as dowry during marriage are very important and get priority and for which they would even incur debt.

The mandal also gives loans for buying bullocks. Under the

tribal sub-plan of the government, tribal farmers are given 50 per cent of the bullock's price as subsidy. Of Rs. 20,000 given by OXFAM forty farmers were given Rs. 500 each to buy a bullock. With great effort the mandal workers got the subsidy from the government for a number of loanees, the total of which amounted to Rs. 8,500. This subsidy was retained by the mandal as part repayment of the loans. The money was let out to seventeen other farmers for buying bullocks. Moreover the mandal had also recovered over Rs. 3,000 from the first round of loans distributed for releasing mortgaged land. This amount was in turn lent to six new farmers for bullocks. Thus the mandal had, in about two years' time, lent more than Rs. 30,000 to sixty-three farmers. The recovery of these loans has not been a major problem as the subsidy received from the government is taken by the mandal as repayment of the loan. However, even after two years some amount from most farmers is still outstanding.

In deciding whom to give loans, the mandal first asked for applications from farmers who had no bullocks. Since applications received outstripped money available, each executive committee member was asked to recommend three names from his village or *falia* (hamlet). Once the recommendations were received, confidential inquiries were made to verify that the persons recommended for loans indeed had no bullocks at all. It was found that in the case of the three recommendations made by one committee member the nominees already had bullocks. Further inquiry revealed that the committee member who had recommended the names actually wanted to sell off the bullocks and share the money with his nominees. The member was removed from the committee and bullocks were not given to his nominees. In order to give loans to more members, each person received only one bullock. Each such loanee would then have to team up with another loanee and borrow each other's bullocks when they needed a pair for tilling land or pulling a cart. For getting the subsidy the mandal leaders themselves prepared all the papers and pursued the matter with the government. The bullocks were also bought by them and given to the loanees instead of giving cash to each member to buy his own bullock.

The mandal also rented out a diesel pump for irrigation at the rate of Rs. 8 per hour with the user bearing the cost of diesel. However, after two years the mandal found that this activity had not proved to be very profitable. Moreover, after the first year they had to send the machine to another village in Dahod taluk, as a large voluntary agency run by a big industrial trust had brought several machines to the village and were renting them out at a highly subsidized rate.

Eight Harijan families were lent Rs. 100 per family to help them in making bamboo baskets. They were to repay Rs. 10 per week. After repaying the first six instalments they have not repaid any money. Four families belonging to the nomadic tribe of Vadis were given Rs. 100 per family to help support their traditional profession of making and selling grain-grinding wheels. However, they have not been able to return any money so far.

Besides such direct economic activities, the mandal has also helped many of the mandal and community members to get the benefit of various governmental programmes for economic development. Some examples are given below:

1. Three villagers were helped to get Rs. 300 each for roof tiles under a scheme of the Social Welfare Department.
2. Under another scheme of the Social Welfare Department, five tuberculosis patients and one leprosy patient were helped to get Rs. 100 per month towards buying medicines and nutritious food.
3. Under the Antyodaya scheme fifteen farmers were helped to get thirty goats.
4. Two farmers were helped to get bullock carts under the tribal development scheme.
5. Under the TRYSEM Programme the mandal arranged for a training programme for brick-making in the village. Forty-five young men of Gamdi and surrounding villages received training.
6. The mandal contacted the forest department and acquired 1,00,000 eucalyptus plants in two instalments for farmers to grow on their farms.

All these activities have required time and consistent effort on the part of mandal workers. For instance, it required getting information, convincing members regarding benefits of various schemes, long and repeated correspondence, repeated trips to government offices and persuading government officials to process papers quickly. Sometimes they had to even prepare all the documents on behalf of government officials so that the officials had only to sign on them. Sometimes, as in the case of applications for the tuberculosis relief scheme, they even had to duplicate application forms as taluk offices would always be short of those. They had to use their high-level political linkages and sometimes even confront the local bureaucracy by asserting their rights or threatening action against them.

Economic Activities through Other Organizations

Besides the activities organized directly under the mandal, mandal leaders have been quite active in starting separate organizations for economic activities. The structure of these organizations is always a cooperative society registered with the Registrar of Cooperative Societies as different from the trust structure of the mandal which is registered with the Charity Commissioner.

In order to get the benefit of many of the economic development programmes of the government, the cooperative society is generally found to be the most suitable form of organization.

Four other cooperative societies are in operation as a spin-off of the mandal's activities. They are:

1. Irrigation Cooperative Society
2. Poultry Farm Cooperative Society
3. Brick Producer's Cooperative Society
4. Milk Producer's Cooperative Society

Besides, mandal members have now taken over control of the existing Agricultural Credit Cooperative Society.

All these societies are managed only by mandal members. Thus the president of the mandal is president of the Irrigation Cooperative. Another executive committee member is president of the Poultry Cooperative. Yet another executive member is secretary of the Agricultural Credit Cooperative.

With these organizations the mandal has been able to extend its interaction and influence within the community on the one hand and with the public administration on the other. It has also brought unprecedented amount of public resources to the villages.

Social Awareness, Social Action and Social Reform Activities

The mandal has been quite active in continuously meeting with, informing and discussing various developmental and social reform issues with young people, women and other community members. The mandal organizes sports activities for the youth and *garbas* (folk dances) for women. The mandal also arranges *bhajan mandalis* every fifteen days in the village. Many people participate in these activities. They utilize these gatherings to discuss issues and problems such as the low level of education among adivasis, the advantages of a small family, immunization and other health services provided by the government, problems of exploitation of adivasis and farmers by traders, politicians and bureaucrats, condition of women in tribal society and evils of bride price. They also inform people about the mandal's activities and its difficulties. They discuss issues relating to the benefits of getting organized.

The mandal workers have not taken up any health or educational activities but exercise vigilance over the government's delivery systems. They visit the village school occasionally and see that teachers open and run the schools regularly. The mandal leaders constantly persuade people to send their children to school. Sometimes when they come to know that a particular child is not attending school or has dropped out they contact the family and see to it that the child is sent back. The bench-mark survey had shown that 174 children of Gamdi village were going to primary school. The leaders claimed that, because of their efforts, in the last two years school attendance had gone up to 240 children.

The mandal workers also keep vigilance over the two community health volunteers, the three *anganwadi* workers (Integrated Child Development Scheme) and the teacher of the nursery school to ensure that they distribute the medicines properly and give meals to the children.

During a short span of three years the mandal had undertaken several fights and agitations for social justice. They were against the exploitation and cheating of tribals, against corruption and irregularity or callousness of the bureaucracy in delivering services. Here are some examples:

1. Three years ago the taluk panchayat president, using his

influence, had got an irrigation scheme for his village supported by a voluntary organization of a large industry. Some people of Gamdi village had lost their lands due to submergence in the small reservoir between Gamdi and the neighbouring village. Moreover the organization had built a dam which prevented Gamdi from getting any irrigation water. The mandal took up the issue, mobilized people to launch satyagraha and threatened to pull down the dam. Since the voluntary organization wanted their scheme to be successful they agreed to start another irrigation scheme for Gamdi using water of the nearby river.

2. The state transport bus service was very irregular and would often altogether miss the scheduled timings. In spite of many applications by the mandal and personal meetings, nothing was done. So the mandal workers called a meeting of Gamdi and neighbouring villages and it was decided to launch an agitation. The mandal workers first took rounds of the neighbouring villages and prepared the people. On the designated day when the bus came it was impounded. People from Gamdi and neighbouring villages numbering 127 participated in the agitation. Senior officers of state transport and police were forced to visit the village. Some people were also arrested. After prolonged negotiations the officials concerned promised to adhere to regular timings and two additional timings were also sanctioned.

Another satyagraha was also successfully carried out to start two new routes.

3. Village Gamdi had a malaria epidemic and five children had died. The malaria supervisor in charge of the village had not been distributing any pills. Moreover, he used to sell off the medicine that he got from the government. He also carried on an illegal private medical practice for which he was not qualified. The mandal workers met the supervisor, his superior officer and the primary health centre doctor. But none of them responded positively to the mandal workers' pleas and petitions, expecting nothing to happen to them.

The mandal workers thereafter met a political leader of the opposition at the district level. He pressurized the police to raid the house of the malaria supervisor, who was immediately transferred and subsequently dismissed. The

whole issue entailed several trips to taluk and district level
offices and meetings with officials of several departments.

4. One of the villagers who had a case filed against him in court
   was forced to give a bribe of Rs. 30 to a policeman and Rs.
   30 to the president of the village panchayat who had acted as
   the middleman. When the villager came to the mandal and
   complained, the leaders contacted the concerned policeman,
   threatened action against him and made both the policeman
   and the *sarpanch* give back the money.

5. The state reserve police (SRP) which was camping near the
   village collected money from the villagers for liquor and
   chicken. The village *sarpanch* had accompanied the SRP.
   The mandal leaders when they came to know about it confronted the SRP and the *sarpanch*. They not only returned
   the money but both were made to apologize.

6. Under the Antyodaya Scheme of the government five villagers
   had been sanctioned grant for housing because of the efforts
   of mandal leaders. This was to be given in instalments. While
   giving the first instalment the concerned official deducted
   some money as his personal commission. When the affected
   villagers approached the mandal leaders they met the concerned official and confronted him. The official agreed to
   return the money to the five villagers. But when the villagers
   met the official he threatened them for having complained to
   the mandal leaders. The mandal leaders again talked to the
   members of the taluk panchayat who were also their executive committee members. The taluk panchayat members re-
   primanded the concerned official and warned him that he
   would be transferred. However, he not only did not return
   the money but held back the second instalment. The mandal
   workers with the support of their taluk panchayat members
   approached the minister at the state level. However, the
   matter had not been resolved till the time of this field work.

7. The Village Level Worker (VLW) who was in charge of
   Gamdi and neighbouring villages was in the habit of taking
   his 'cut' since he was the official to process all applications
   for getting the benefits of various developmental schemes.
   Once he had taken Rs. 50 from a farmer for getting him the
   subsidy for a bullock under the IRDP and Rs. 100 from
   another farmer for the subsidy for a diesel engine. Both the

affected farmers complained to mandal workers. Mandal members contacted the VLW who said that he had not taken the money but given it to the veterinary doctor who certified the bullock for insurance and to the loans distribution officer who had released the instalment for the diesel engine. But the mandal leaders pressurized him to return the money and told him that since he was an adivasi they would not complain against him but he should, however, stop taking bribes.

These are some examples of mandal leaders taking action against extortion, exploitation and injustice. Mandal leaders feel that it has made considerable impact on the local administration and others who exploit adivasis. They claim that they have now virtually eliminated petty corruption of local administration in their villages and the local administration now respond to their demands promptly and carefully.

Another major activity that they have taken up is social reform. We have already mentioned their attempts at bringing social awareness. A major component of their social awareness activities is social reform and change among their own people. These deal with persuading their community members not to demand or give dowry in marriage, not to enter into quarrels and feuds, not to spend beyond their capacity on marriage and death ceremonies, not to take recourse to faith healers and witch doctors at the time of disease or some other calamity in the family, to give up child marriage and give up drinking liquor (which they believe is the major cause of the poverty, misery and exploitation of adivasis). In Gamdi village there were seven distillers, who sold liquor. The mandal had offered them free buffaloes if they agreed to change over to selling milk instead of liquor. One of them accepted the mandal's offer and stopped selling liquor. According to mandal leaders, incidence of drinking in their villages has reduced considerably because of their efforts. The Gamdi mandal runs its own courts called *Nyaya Panch* (Justice Commission).

'Adivasi society is full of quarrels, feuds and rivalries,' said the president of the Gamdi mandal. 'We ruin ourselves with these feuds and rivalries'. Quarrels are mainly centred around women and land. This is also one of the major causes of adivasis' exploitation. When these feuds and rivalries take place between two families or members of the same family, the traditional tribal leaders act as arbitrators and negotiators. The solutions offered by them are often not just. The one who is willing to spend more money or offer them money gets the decision in his favour. The solutions are in keeping with traditional customs which the arbitrators try to zealously reinforce, without caring whether it financially ruins the contestants. If either party decides to take the matter to court, then too the leaders act as go-between for the party concerned and the police or court officials. They accompany him to the town where police or courts are located at his expense which includes bus fare, snacks or meals, smokes and so on. They settle with the police and other officials the amount of bribes (sometimes the amount taken is more than what is actually paid and the difference is pocketed), arrange for lawyers, loans and mortgages of land. They may also take personal cuts and besides have to be wined and dined at the end. All this would normally push the litigant towards debt and financial ruin.

With the first OXFAM grant of Rs. 1,500 for training, two of the mandal's workers had visited various development projects and voluntary organizations in Gujarat. One such visit was to Anand Niketan Ashram in Baroda district which has been operating *lok adalats* (people's court) for many years. The purpose of the *lok adalat* is to dissuade adivasis from going to courts for settling disputes and to dispense quick justice with minimum expense without pushing the adivasis further into debt.

After observing this experiment the Gamdi mandal took up the activity. The three members of the mandal who are usually active in this work are the president, secretary and the treasurer. The mandal's record with this activity has been quite good. In less than three years' time they have tackled nearly 100 disputes.

They handle the cases very tactfully and come up with creative solutions. Since the feuding parties belong to their village and are known to them or in some cases are related to them they have to be very careful. For instance, before the court is held they would study the case, find out the details of the problem and also the motives of the parties concerned. They would try to ascertain which person has been advising or supporting the parties concerned. They would also try and identify the person who has some influence or hold over the families of the parties concerned, and if useful, invite him to remain present so that he can help.

In the initial stages they also invited the traditional leaders, so as not to go against them and create internal rivalries within the village. However, during the proceedings they would handle the matters in such a way that the traditional leaders did not have much say or influence. After a while the latter, when they saw that they had no role, stopped attending. But in the beginning, after the disputes were settled, the traditional leaders went to the concerned parties in the evening and demanded liquor and mutton; but after a while people refused to submit to their demands.

In order to reduce undue influence of traditional leaders and their exploitation, one of the strategies adopted by the mandal was to hold the court in public and make the proceedings open, where at least thirty-five to forty other villagers would also be present. This would also put some social pressure both on the defaulting party and the aggrieved party to come to some solution.

While dispensing justice the mandal sees to it that no party is put under financial strain. The guilty party is only charged a small fine. This amount is immediately spent in buying jaggery and coconut and distributed on the spot to the people present and children in the village. This has enhanced the credibility of the mandal and its leaders because people see that they personally do not take any money.

Secondly, they try to bring about an amicable solution and also see to it that rivalries do not continue. For instance, the president told us that in many cases of marital disputes, the husband and wife do not have any problems. It is the elders in the family who create dissension among the couple. The real quarrel may not be between the husband and wife at all but between the wife and her husband's family. Sometimes it is the elders who may want the man to get divorced and remarry or marry a second wife. The man concerned may not be able to resist because of the pressure of the elders. In such cases, the *nyaya panch* persuades the elders or even exposes them and tries to prevent the separation or second marriage.

While dispensing justice they also keep in mind the social reform aspect. In running the *nyaya panch* every opportunity is used to bring about social change or reform. A couple of examples of this type of mediation activity by the Gamdi Mandal are discussed in Chapter 6.

As a result of this activity the villagers now come to the mandal leaders for advice on buying or selling land or ornaments, settling marriages and decision on types of crops to grow. They now increasingly consult mandal leaders before entering into any major financial transaction to ensure that they are not cheated or exploited.

Political Activities

This is one of the few groups which directly and intensively participates in electoral and partisan political activities. They have mainly taken an active part in having some of their men as representatives in village, taluk and district panchayat bodies.

Some examples of the mandal's thinking and manner of participation in electoral politics are discussed in Chapter 7. The mandal leaders have also built up strong linkages with the Member of Parliament from their area, and the state-level minister from their district. They are not very happy with the member of the state assembly representing their constituency. They feel that he is not active in solving the problems of the people of their area and does not actively help and support the activities of the mandal. The mandal leaders said that in the next state assembly elections they will represent before the Congress Party not to give him the ticket and if in spite of their representation if he is given the ticket they will oppose him.

In getting involved in political activities, the mandal is not partisan in the sense that they are not committed to any one party. They emphasize the person rather than the party. This is evident from the stand that the mandal has taken, in the examples described in Chapter 7. It is also evident from the fact that two of its executive committee members are members of the taluk panchayat from two different political parties. However, they always operate through some political party or the other.

Mandal leaders say that they would support those candidates or representatives who would do 'our work'. By 'our' they mean primarily the work of the people of the villages covered by the mandal and tribals of their area in general. Most work consists of getting speedier sanctions, permissions, loans, subsidies and benefits of development schemes and programmes. What it essentially boils down to is to prevail upon the politicians to use their power and influence to pressurize political and public administration institutions in their favour rather than somebody else's favour.

The mandal's political work consists of influencing the taluk or district administrative system and the political process in general to improve their performance, to become less corrupt and more people-oriented or poor-oriented. The president said, for instance, that in all the subsequent elections of the local bodies and the state assembly they would put up a candidate. 'We will select a person who is honest and who is capable of getting "our work" done from the government departments.'

The mandal leaders say that politicians have begun to notice them. The politicians are also worried that if the mandal becomes very successful and popular then they will have difficulty in winning elections. They may begin to intervene in the mandal's work and try to create rivalries and factions among the mandal leaders.

> We are, therefore, working very tactfully and we adopt different strategies so that they do not become successful in creating factions among us. Before taking up any major social action issue we first discuss among ourselves and decide which political leader to consult and approach for support.

At the moment the mandal leaders feel that they have strong influence over the people of the area and, therefore, if their candidate turns out to be dishonest, selfish or corrupt they will be able to defeat him.[1] They feel confident that they will be able to handle the politicians.

Extension, Linkages and Network

The mandal has also tried to extend itself beyond its own area and has shown some interest in issues which are not merely local.

The grant of Rs. 1,500 given by OXFAM for training has been used by the mandal members to send some of its office bearers to visit various other voluntary action projects in Gujarat and Maharashtra. The women were also sent to Ahmedabad's SEWA (Self Employed Women's Association) for training in organizing women's activities. The mandal office bearers have attended virtually all the *shibirs* organized for small action groups in Gujarat.

---

[1] This seems to be over-confidence. In the 1987 Panchayat elections the president of the Gamdi mandal contested at taluk and district levels as an independent candidate and lost both the elections.

Several of the mandal's office bearers played a very active role in organizing a state-wide *shibir* of small action groups in the summer of 1984.

When OXFAM did not give any funds to a proposed women's organization at Gamdi, the Gamdi Yuvak Mandal helped them to get registered and advanced them Rs. 2,000 to start some activities.

Similarly, mandal leaders and particularly its president Bhalabhai, have played very active roles in helping several other small groups to get organized. Beside giving them information and guidance they have also helped them to find sources of funds. The mandal leaders are in contact with most other groups in Panchmahals district. In our discussion, the president could give us detailed information about the situation of other groups in Panchmahals.

Panchmahals district groups, with the help of OXFAM funding, have federated into a district-level association of adivasi youth organizations called *Panchmahals District Adivasi Yuvak Mandal Sangh*. Bhalabhai, the president of the Gamdi Yuvak Mandal, is taking a lead in the activities of this federation. He is also its secretary.[2] This district-level association has made considerable progress and has taken up quite a few activities in the last two years.

The leaders of the Gamdi Yuvak Mandal have also cooperated and participated actively in the larger problems of tribals at higher levels. The mandal leaders supported and participated actively in the rally organized at Zalod town to counter the anti-reservation movement of the upper castes. They also participated in meetings and the rally to protest against the Forest Policy Bill of the government.

In March 1983, a major convention was organized by the joint efforts of the Panchmahals Yuvak Mandals, to put before the state government some 'burning problems' of the tribals of Panchmahals. This was done in collaboration with a regional political party. The leaders of the Gamdi mandal had taken an active part in helping to organize the convention which was attended by nearly 10,000 tribals.

[2] He subsequently became coordinator of the association with a regular monthly salary from OXFAM.

We have noted that the mandal has established strong linkages with some district and state-level political leaders. The mandal has also established contact with more established voluntary action groups and activists from other areas. Thus the Gamdi mandal's network of linkages and involvement with the problems of tribals is quite extensive and strong for a small and young group.

Difficulties and Impediments

Among the major difficulties that the Gamdi mandal has faced is resistance from the established leaders of the older generation from their own villages. Generally, these traditional and established leaders collaborate with outside exploiters and help facilitate cheating, exploitation, and sometimes even physical oppression. This they are able to do because of their access to bureaucracy, and other outside groups like businessmen, contractors and police and also because of their hold over their own people. Their own traditional control and influence over the people is enhanced by their access to and influence with modern institutions. Gamdi mandal's activities have not been liked by the established leaders, particularly the ex-*sarpanch* of the village panchayat. However, without confronting them but by organizing people and undertaking their activities successfully the mandal has been able to reduce the control and influence of these traditional leaders in the community. Yet, if they make a major mistake or meet with failure in any of their activities then there is every likelihood of these traditional leaders maligning them and spreading rumours against them.

Secondly, while Gamdi mandal has taken up many activities and brought considerable resources to the village through various co-operatives that they have started, they still face the problem of general or unattached funds of their own. In more than three years of its activities the mandal has generated only small amount of its own funds. We have noted that while members and villagers participate quite actively and have benefited a lot, they are not willing to support the mandal financially. Even a meagre membership fee of Rs. 5 in two years is given reluctantly and there is a considerable incidence of default. The mandal also has some difficulty in timely recovery of loans advanced to their members.

Thirdly, the bureaucracy's response to the mandal's activities and demands is lukewarm. Mandal leaders have to go often and repeatedly to taluk and district offices to get things done. For a small matter they must meet many officers and even activate contacts with politicians. The mandal has some members and villagers in government service as are members and office bearers of other groups too. The mandal tries to use all these connections to get work done from the administration. Because of these linkages and sustained and determined efforts the mandal has been generally successful in getting things done from the bureaucracy. But, repeated trips and having to pressurize, cajole or threaten the bureaucracy frequently is time consuming, expensive and exhausting.

Whenever they have confronted corrupt or irresponsible officials, the latter have generally retreated and given in, but sometimes they have also harassed the mandal. In the case of subsidies for bullocks, though it was given initially later on the administration stopped it on the ground that only those farmers would get the subsidy who take the loans from banks and not from the mandal. They also raised questions about the legal status of the mandal for distributing loans and a police inquiry was made. The mandal leaders felt that this was done to demoralize them and to tarnish their image before the mandal and community members.

These then are some of the difficulties and impediments that the mandal is facing. Their greatest worry is however, a possibility of internal strife and factionalism. They feel that with increasing economic activities, people with ulterior motives will try to capture the mandal with support from outside politicians and the local bureaucracy. So far however, they have been able to contain divisive forces effectively.

Impact

The mandal's economic activities seem to have made noticeable impact.

1. Members who had received subsidies for a bullock or got water through the mandal's diesel pump and later through the irrigation cooperative society, whom we could interview, all categorically stated that their agricultural production had gone up. It is difficult to say exactly how much production

had increased but when asked they talked of double and three-fold increase in production.

2. Those who had got back their mortgaged land also asserted that they had received great economic help.
3. Another important achievement has been the proper utilization of loans advanced by the mandal. The mandal leaders, by repeated visits, enquiries and constant monitoring, ensured that the money was utilized by those in whose names they were taken, and for the purpose for which the loan was advanced. Proper utilization of loans was nearly 100 per cent.
4. The mandal leaders said that because of its economic activities, particularly release of mortgaged land and irrigation, there was noticeable decrease in the incidence of migration. The president, who has a good sense for quantitative data and is quite particular about facts and figures, stated that migration in Gamdi was reduced by 20 per cent.
5. More importantly, the mandal's economic activities had for the first time reached the very poor people and what are known as the bottom 20 per cent. As stated earlier, the criteria that the mandal set for advancing loans were such that the very poor and needy were given preference.

In Gamdi village, the mandal has reached practically every family that they considered very poor through its economic activities. In other villages also, within the mandal's sphere of activities, they first tried to help the very poor. No other programme of the government or any other public institution in the last thirty-five years has ever reached the kind of poor people that the mandal has reached in Gamdi.

Its political activities has made the mandal a political force in the area. It has now been well accepted by the people in the eight or ten villages surrounding the mandal. And even beyond these villages mandal leaders hold considerable political influence with the people.

1. This has encouraged the mandal to impress upon local political leaders to be honest and active in solving people's problems. The mandal leaders have also got them to visit their villages more often than before.

2. It has also influenced the local bureaucracy who are now aware of the mandal's political power.

3. They have also constantly and repeatedly impressed upon the people that only people-oriented and honest politicians should be supported. As a result both politicians and bureaucrats are quite careful in dealing with mandal members and mandal villages and generally respond to their demands.

4. The mandal's leaders claim that because of their social action activities they have been very successful in virtually eradicating the petty corruption of local level officials. The *talati*, village level worker, police and forest beat guard do not dare to threaten people, harass women or extort money, grains or chicken. All the other people of the village that we talked to also said that officials do not demand any bribes from them and they are able to get their work done much more easily than before.

The mandal's activities has made the community quite powerful and 'significant' in the eyes of politicians and bureaucrats. The attention, services and response that they have received in the last three years far exceeds anything they had ever received before. The *talati*, the VLW, anganwadi workers, school teachers, health workers, community health volunteer of village Gamdi are all working more regularly. The exposure to and interaction of the community with the outside world, the higher and more important levels of politics and administration, has increased considerably.

On the one hand, while they have been quite successful in taking on outside politicians and administrators, on the other they have also been successful in reducing the power and hold of entrenched interests and the traditional leadership within their own communities, who generally collaborate with outside politicians, bureaucrats and businessmen in cheating and exploiting the poor.

The active members of the mandal—the office holders, the executive committee members and the few ordinary actively involved members have acquired knowledge and information, an understanding of the social structure, political processes and the nature of exploitation. They have learned skills in mobilization and organization that they admit they never thought themselves capable of.

The mandal members and the community have now acquired considerable confidence that they can deal with their problems, that they have the skills, capabilities and the resource to fight their oppressors—the politician, the police, the *patwari* or their own police patel. They do not feel that sense of total helplessness against internal or external exploiters. It is in this sense that the Gamdi Vibhag Adivasi Yuvak Mandal has made its community powerful.

9

The Abhlod Yuvak Mandal[1]

Abhlod Yuvak Mandal is situated in Abhlod village of Dahod Taluk in Panchmahals district. Besides Abhlod it covers four other villages. The names of the villages and number of households covered by Abhlod Yuvak Mandal as well as major castes are given below:

Village	Approximate Number of Households in the Village	Major Castes
Abhlod	950	Adivasi, Bharwad, Harijans
Paneldi	234	Adivasi, Patidar
Vijagadh	304	Adivasi
Gadoi	225	Adivasi
Khajuria	185	Adivasi

The major castes in Abhlod village are tribals (about 75 per cent) and Bharwads (about 20 per cent). There are two divisions among the tribals in the area—Patelia and Bhil. These two sub-tribes do not intermarry but they do have dining relations. Patelias are economically and educationally better off than Bhils. They own more land and are generally recognized as more advanced and higher up the social scale. Bhils, while they do own some land, have also to migrate seasonally for labour. They are poorer and backward as compared to Patelias.

Besides adivasis and Bharwads there are quite a few households of scheduled castes (seventeen in Abhlod) and Patidars, who are landlords and money-lenders. The local shopkeepers in these villages are generally Vohras, a Muslim sect. They sell daily

---

[1] A modified version of this case in a different framework has been published in Anil Bhatt et al., Building from Below, op. cit. pp. 237–66.

necessities including clothes. They lend money and give food-grains, cloth and other household necessities on credit against land and ornaments.

Abhlod, where most of the activities of the mandal is concentrated has a nursery school, pre-primary and primary school and two high schools. One of the two high schools is an Ashramshala run by the Panchmahals District Bhil Seva Mandal.[2] The other high school has started recently and is managed by the mandal. There is a group village panchayat located at Abhlod. There are also irrigation and poultry cooperative societies in Abhlod managed by the mandal.

Genesis

The Abhlod Yuvak Mandal was one of the earliest to get started among the small action groups that we have studied. It was formed in 1972 and was registered with the Charity Commissioner in August 1974.

The man to start this mandal was the father of the present president of the mandal. He was police patel of this village. A leader of the village with primary education, he was interested in public and political activities. In order to start some activities in the village he formed the Abhlod Yuvak Mandal in 1974. At the time he got elected to the taluk panchayat as the candidate of the then Congress party. He is currently a member of the district panchayat from the Congress (I) party. The idea of forming a village level mandal was suggested to him by a VLW who told him that if a mandal was formed it would be more effective in getting benefits of development from government schemes and projects. Initially, the mandal took up the activity of *nyaya panchayat* and running adult education classes at night. It also took up night patrolling of the village to protect against the menace of dacoits. Funds were also collected from the villagers to build a temple. However, this mandal soon became defunct. Most older members lost interest and became inactive.

In 1979, his son who was working in the telephones department was transferred to Panchmahals district. While his job was in

---

[2] It is one of the large and well-established voluntary organisations in Panch-mahals district. It has been involved in educational and other developmental activities among the tribals for more than sixty years.

Dahod town he stayed in village Abhlod from where he used to commute. At about the same time Bhalabhai Raval, the present president of Gamdi Mandal (see Chapter 8 on Gamdi Mandal) was posted in Abhlod as vaccinator. Bhalabhai was very active in youth activities and he had earlier formed such a mandal in Kanjetha, where he had been working. He was also a secretary of the Panchmahals Zilla Adivasi Yuvak Mandal at Zalod.

Bhalabhai formed a cricket team in the village which attracted young and educated members of the community. Most of them were either government employees or traders. The son of the then president also joined the cricket team. He talked to Bhalabhai about the Abhlod Yuvak Mandal which had by then become totally defunct. He also told him that the accounts of the mandal were not prepared and audited and that the Charity Commissioner's office was demanding the audited statement of accounts.

Bhalabhai sorted out the accounts, prepared a statement of accounts and got them audited. They then thought of reviving the mandal. The executive committee was completely changed. Most of the new members were young and well-known to each other as members of the cricket team.

They first went from house to house and discussed with the people village problems like internal disputes, court cases and harassment from *talati* and police. People from nearby villages were also contacted and asked to join the mandal. Bhalabhai, who had now become the treasurer, of the newly revived Abhlod mandal knew about the OXFAM programme of helping small village level organizations, because of his experience with the Panchmahals Zilla Mandal to which OXFAM had given funds. They decided to approach OXFAM for help. Thus the mandal was formed and revived. It soon became one of the very active small action groups in the tribal areas of Gujarat.

Funding

The mandal, when it was revived in 1980, took Rs. 10 from each member as, what it calls, share fee (though the mandal has not issued any share certificates as it is not a cooperative society). Thus Rs. 10 was some sort of an initial entrance fee. Rs. 2 per member was taken as membership fee. Though this membership fee is to be taken annually the mandal has taken this fee only once in four years. This is so because members are not very regular in giving their membership dues and are generally reluctant to make financial contributions, though both mandal members as well as villagers contributed readily and generously when the mandal appealed to them for funds to renovate the village temple.

This group has received the highest amount of OXFAM funds. In about one and half years between May 1981 to September 1982, OXFAM has given funds totalling more than Rs. 70,000 for various activities as detailed below:

Amount (Rs.)	Purpose
16,000	Well deepening
4,000	Seeds distribution for members of Khajuria Village
10,000	Seeds distribution
10,500	For buying diesel oil engine
30,000	For buying bullocks
70,500	**Total**

After September 1982 OXFAM has not given any funds to this mandal.

The mandal has also tried to generate its own funds but has not been very successful. For instance, it started a lottery but because of the propaganda against it by some school teachers in the village, many people did not buy tickets and the mandal leaders had to bear the loss from their own pocket.

The mandal's record of accounts and management of funds are reasonably well maintained and quite up to date. However, the office bearers of the mandal do not have a clear idea of their own general funds in addition to the activity-specific funds given by an outside agency.

Membership and Leadership

When the mandal's activities were revived the leaders who had taken the initiative launched a membership drive. Earlier, the mandal had no members or membership fee or any formal enrollment of members. In 1980, the mandal leaders started enrollment with a membership fee of Rs. 2 per year. Within two years they had 235 members. Village-wise membership is as follows:

Village	Number of Members	Proportion of Tribal Members
Abhlod	150	84%
Gadoi	10	80%
Vijagadh	10	100%
Paneldi	15	100%
Khajuria	50	100%
Total	235	

A large number of members are from Abhlod village. Khajuria has the next highest number of members. That is because a specific amount was given by OXFAM for loans to people of Khajuria village which enhanced the membership. Since all these areas are predominantly inhabited by adivasis they constitute a majority of the members. Abhlod has twenty members of the Bharwad caste belonging to the backward groups as scheduled by the Baxi Panch. It also has four scheduled caste members.

Though these villages have a few households of forward groups like Banias, Patels, Sindhis and Vohras, they are not encouraged to join the mandal unless where the mandal leaders know them personally. For instance, four of the 235 members are from forward groups of Panchals, Sindhis and Banias. All four of them are also executive committee members. But they were taken because they had shown some interest in the mandal's activities and were personally known to the president and secretary.

Background information on the executive committee members is given in Table 11.

This is one of the very few groups where except one executive committee member all have high school education or are college graduates. Also, this is the only mandal where only one executive member is a farmer while all others are either in business, private practice or government service besides owning some land. As can be seen from the information on the executive committee, like the Gamdi group, this group also has executive members occupying important leadership positions in other village level organizations. But they owed these positions to their work in the mandal.

The relationship between members and leaders is generally good and cooperative. The general meeting is formally held once a year at the time of giving loans, but informal meetings for discussion are held whenever the mandal takes up some new activity

TABLE 11

The Executive Committee of the Abhlod Yuvak Mandal

Position	Age	Education	Occupation	Caste	Land	Other information
President	35	SSC	Technician in Post & Telegraphs	Tribal	5 acres	President Panchmahals Zilla Sangh
Vice-President	33	SSC	Shopkeeper	Baxi	—	—
Vice-President	32	SSC	Agriculture	Bharwad	2 acres	—
Secretary	31	SSC	Service	Blacksmith	2 acres	—
Dy. Secretary*	23	SSC	Clerk in High School	Bharwad	3 acres	Dy. Sarpanch
Treasurer	36	SSC	Vaccinator	Tribal	—	Secretary Panchmahals Zilla Sangh
Member	37	SSC	Business	Blacksmith	5 acres	—
Member	37	BA, LLB	Doctor	Bania	—	—
Member	38	SSC	Doctor	Sindhi	—	—
Member	36	SSC	Ration Shop	Tribal	5 acres	—
Member	35	9th Std.	Shop	Bharwad	5 acres	—

* Since the collection of this information the deputy secretary was killed while fighting dacoits. Bania and Sindhi members were asked to leave the mandal as they were not very active.

or an important village level problem. Moreover, besides marriages, *bhajan mandalis* and religious occasions, the leaders and members also get together at the meetings of other organizations like the irrigation and poultry cooperatives started by the mandal.

Because of the many social action activities handled by this group, participation and involvement of ordinary members is high.

Membership fee is collected from individual members at the time of recovery of loans. However, members of other villages seem to have lost interest after they got their loans. Khajuria village members for whom OXFAM had given specific grant are not renewing their membership nor are they returning the loans. In fact at present the mandal leaders are not interacting a great deal with the Khajuria village members. This is also due to the fact that during the recent attack of the dacoits on Abhlod village, it was suspected that some of the dacoits were from Khajuria. In the case of other villages also interaction has dwindled to only two or three members.

Most decisions about new activities or loans are taken in the general meeting; however, the leading decision makers are office bearers of the mandal.

Economic Activities

As mentioned earlier, among all the OXFAM supported groups, this mandal has received maximum funds. The major economic activities that the mandal performs directly with its own funds are: loans for deepening wells, buying seeds, buying bullocks and irrigation with the diesel oil pump bought by the mandal with an OXFAM grant.

So far more than 108 members have been given seed loans besides fifty members of Khajuria village. Most of these members were given loans for seeds two to three times in the last three years while a few members have got it only once. The loan money, whenever recovered, is revolved every year. The seed loan is generally given repeatedly to the same member unless the member does not want it or if he is a defaulter in terms of repayment.

In case of the diesel oil pump, whoever requires water is loaned the pump at rates varying between Rs. 20 and Rs. 25 an hour. The loan for bullocks was given to sixty members of whom fifty-four were tribals and six were Bharwads. For giving loans applications were asked for. Nearly 200 applications were received. A committee consisting of one executive committee member and two advisory members, including a harijan, was formed. The committee also included two members from each *falia* to review applicants from their respective falias. The criteria for selection of loanees stipulated that he had to be a member of the mandal and not have more than one bullock. Preference was given to the very poor and needy farmers who had no bullock of their own. The committee visited each household and gave the money in two instalments. The second instalment was given only after the bullock was purchased.

The mandal also collaborated with the bank to get loans for bullocks for which subsidies from the IRDP programme was available. Fifty-six farmers were helped in preparing applications for the loans and subsidies.

A similar procedure was followed for well-deepening loans. Fifty-three applications were received. The committee visited each of the fifty-three applicants. The committee, besides ascertaining the financial condition of the farmer and his real need, also ascertained whether the farmer would get more water after deepening the well, whether he was willing to do the work himself and was keen to finish it. Thirty-four farmers were selected. Another group of eight farmers were given loans for well deepening in the second year, out of the recovery of the first round of loans.

While repaying the loan each loanee had to give Rs. 10 extra from which his membership dues were deducted and the rest remained with the mandal as mandal funds to be used for administrative expenses.

The mandal members face some difficulty in the recovery of loans, as they have to repeatedly remind the farmers and it sometimes spoil their relations with their own community members. Even those who repay rarely repay in time. They have been able to recover only 10 per cent of the loan amount distributed to members of Khajuria village. Out of Rs. 70,500 lent so far the mandal has recovered about Rs. 23,000, which is one third of the total amount lent for various purposes.

Social Awareness, Social Reform and Social Action Activities

Like Gamdi, Abhlod Yuvak Mandal has also carried out many

social development and social action activities against injustice, irregularity and corruption.

The mandal leaders regularly participate in *bhajan mandalis* and religious gatherings. They also arrange folk dances during the Navratri festival. During these gatherings they talk about the mandal's activities, discuss about recovery of loans, about other development activities and problems of the village. They try to educate people on health, family planning and education.

The mandal has been very active in the educational field. They had been trying to get a sanction for a pre-primary school for the village from the Social Welfare Department since 1982; and finally got the approval at the beginning of 1985.

The mandal has also written to the Social Welfare Department for starting training classes in carpentary and sewing classes for women. They are persuing the matter but have not been successful so far.

Abhlod has a post-basic Ashram school. The school is up to the 10th grade of the secondary school system and has a hostel for the students. According to mandal leaders the school was not being run regularly. The results of the final secondary school examination of this school was very poor. The teachers and headmaster would be absent for days together. The school has thirteen acres of land donated by the village. The produce of the land, according to mandal leaders, was being misappropriated by the teachers and the students were not given enough and good food. The students were not given clothing regularly even though the government gives grant for food and clothing of adivasi students. Often students were called away from their classes to do domestic work in the teachers' houses. The mandal leaders tried to bring this to the notice of the principal. They started visiting the school and demanded access to the attendance register and the stock of foodgrains for students. They were successful in getting transferred two wardens of the hostel who were selling foodgrains meant for the students.

Finally, the mandal leaders approached another statewide organization, the Khetvikas Parishad at Ahmedabad, to start a school in their village. The Khetvikas Parishad subsequently started a school which is supported and virtually managed by the Abhlod mandal. The joint secretary of the mandal became a clerk in the school. In order to start the school the mandal leaders initially lent their own money and recovered it after the government grant was given. Although the school is sponsored by the Khetvikas Parishad, it is managed by the Abhlod mandal. The Khetvikas Parishad has now agreed in principle to hand over the school formally to the mandal. According to the mandal leaders it was only formally undertaken by the Parishad in order to facilitate getting the government sanction; in reality the mandal was managing everything.

The Abhlod Yuvak Mandal has undertaken the major activity of getting the cultivable land of Abhlod and its neighbouring villages irrigated. They feel that irrigation is the major input needed for better agriculture. It would also, they argue, stop migration and reduce poverty. By their efforts they have been able to get work related to irrigation started by the government from two ponds and a river in and around Abhlod. These are all small irrigation schemes and expected to irrigate nearly 50 per cent of the cultivable land in Abhlod village besides some land in the neighbouring villages. They had to, however, struggle hard to get these schemes started. One of the irrigation projects was supposed to have been completed and functioning more than three decades ago, according to government records. But in reality both the work of the dam as well as the canal was left incomplete. The mandal took up this issue. They sent applications to the government under the government's Small Irrigation Scheme, Drought-prone Area Programme, district panchayat and every scheme or department which they thought may have something to do with irrigation.

When the mandal took up the issue their interest and locus standi was questioned by the government. But the father of the president of the mandal, who is an elected member of the district panchayat and a member of the ruling party, also pursued the matter with the government. So the officers had to listen to the representatives made by mandal leaders. The mandal leaders went on pursuing the matter for nearly one and half years. They visited the taluk and district offices as many as twenty to twenty-five times. They took up the matter at the state level through their representatives in the state assembly and ultimately influenced the minister for irrigation, who was a tribal, to issue orders to take up the matter.

When the sanction was given by the government they relentlessly pursued the officers to start the work immediately. When the work started the mandal leaders kept constant vigilance on the contractor to see that he did the work according to specifications and used good quality material. (Once they sent a sample of the materials used by the contractor to the taluk office to stop him from using poor quality material.) But they also provided help for speeding up the work. They mobilized labour from the village when the contractor who had undertaken the work disappeared without completing it. During the visits of the officers they provided hospitality and made arrangements for their overnight stay so that the work would be completed quickly. Their efforts paid off, they got the dam and the canal constructed; which on government records was already completed more than thirty years ago!

Like the Gamdi mandal, the Abhlod mandal has also taken up many issues with the local bureaucracy regarding corruption and harassment of villagers by village and other government functionaries, which generally consist of insulting them, making them visit repeatedly, not providing them adequate or correct information or even deliberately giving them wrong information. Thus the mandal repeatedly, and almost always successfully, fought *talatis*, village level workers, the veterinary doctor (who was doing private practice and charging a fee) and other local officials. The mandal leaders were successful in getting corrupt local officials transferred or suspended by writing to their superiors, insisting upon official inquiries and sometimes getting them trapped by the Anti-Corruption Bureau.

The mandal has carried out three satyagrahas in which more than 100 people from the village participated. Two of these satyagrahas were against the State Transport Corporation to get them to regularize and increase bus services. One was against the Public Works Department to get the approach road to the village repaired which was already sanctioned by the zilla panchayat but was not being done.

The mandal has also been able to keep considerable vigilance and check on the village panchayat whose *sarpanch*, they allege, was very corrupt. Because the mandal's joint secretary is also a deputy *sarpanch*, he has successfully protested against the *sarpanch* getting bogus vouchers and bills sanctioned by the panchayat.

The mandal has taken up the issue of thirty-two farmers who were given some forest land by the government because they had lost their land through submergence in a government irrigation scheme. Since the government procedure of transferring the forest land in their name in government records was delayed, the forest department took away this land where they developed a nursery. The mandal had to fight hard and relentlessly all the way up to the state level for three years to get back the land and return it to the farmers.

While the mandal fights corruption in the local government, they also help and support local officials to get the work of their community members expedited. Thus they approach officials to visit their village frequently and provide them hospitality to get the work of the community members done smoothly and quickly. The mandal leaders claim that officials up to the district level now know them well and are scared of them so they do not indulge in any corruption in their village and the surrounding areas. Moreover, this repeated interaction with bureaucracy has also given them considerable courage and confidence. They are no more afraid to straightaway approach the district collector, the highest official of the district.

The Abhlod Yuvak Mandal has also undertaken social reform activities. During their meetings and gatherings with members and other villagers they constantly discuss the harmful effects of drinking. They talk of the exploitative role of the traditional tribal leaders, arbitrators and negotiators. They tell people not to spend too much on marriages and death rituals, not to have more than one wife and so on.

Their social reform work has induced mandal leaders to expand their activities beyond the few villages and cover the whole area of social interaction of their tribal group. With the help of another mandal at Kharoda village a major caste conference was organized. This was attended by young men and caste leaders and elders of nearly forty tribal villages. The Abhlod leaders, along with many other young men, were successful in making the caste conference take decisions regarding marriage and other social customs.[3]

Political Activity

The Abhlod Yuvak Mandal is politically quite active. It has all

---

[3] Some of these are described in Chapter 6.

along supported the Congress and later the Congress (I) Party. As noted earlier, the first president of the mandal and the father of the present president is a member of the Zilla Panchayat on a Congress (I) ticket.

The mandal also tries to get Congress tickets for what they call 'their men' (i.e., those who are in contact with mandal leaders and would support and favour them), in local government elections. Mandal leaders have close contact with one state assembly representative of their constituency who is also a minister. He visits the village frequently and generally stays at the mandal president's house. During elections mandal leaders canvass for the Congress (I) Party in their individual capacity but try to impress upon the people that if they vote for the candidate for whom they are canvassing, the mandal's and the people's work would get easily done. During the parliamentary elections held in December 1984, some of the mandal leaders actively canvassed for the Congress (I) party. They claimed that there was a lot of support for the Janata Party candidate among the people of the area but it was because of their efforts that the tables were turned in favour of the Congress (I) Party.

Spin-off Organizations

Because of the efforts of the mandal three cooperative societies have been started. The irrigation activities started in a big way in the last three years has led the mandal to take a major lead in forming an irrigation cooperative.

The mandal has also formed a milk producers cooperative society. It has 138 members. Because of the mandal's efforts fifty-three tribal members of the society got buffaloes from the Tribal Development Corporation.

Taking advantage of the location of a branch office of the Tribal Development Corporation in a nearby town, mandal leaders took active part in organizing the people into a poultry cooperative. The mandal, under its auspices, carried out all correspondence and contacted the concerned officers on behalf of members of the society. The poultry society has seventy members and has received poultry and cages worth Rs. 19,000, by way of an initial grant, from the Tribal Development Corporation.

Many villagers from Abhlod have been members of the Agricultural Credit Cooperative Society in Jesawada village, nearly twenty kilometers from Abhlod. The villagers had to travel that distance, sometimes repeatedly, for getting credit and bringing seeds and fertilizers etc. Mandal leaders were successful in getting a branch of the society opened in their village.

The new school that the mandal started and is managing has already been referred to earlier.

Linkages

The Abhlod Yuvak Mandal has built up many linkages with the outside world. Through other adivasi employees of their own mandal and the village and through other mandals they have been able to develop many contacts in various government departments up to the district level.

The mandal leaders have attended most training camps organized by OXFAM, SETU and other organizations.

The mandal leaders are in close touch with other similar groups of the district. There is particularly close interaction with groups of the Zalod and Dahod taluks. Often the leaders of two or three mandals go together to the district or state level offices when they have some work. The president of the Abhlod mandal is also the president of the district level association of these small groups. As mentioned earlier, the treasurer of the mandal is a president of the Gamdi Yuvak Mandal and secretary of the district association of these groups.

The mandal has strong political linkages at the taluk, district and state levels as described in the section on Political Activities.

Difficulties and Dangers

When the mandal began its activities the major difficulties they faced were both internal and external. The external difficulties were mainly from the local administration who would not respond to the mandal's demands and who would question the locus standi of the mandal for taking up matters with them. However, because of their perseverance, determination to fight and even organize mass agitation if necessary and because of their administrative and political linkages they have generally been able to make the administration respond to their needs and demands.

Their major internal difficulty is opposition from within the community, from people who do not like their activities or whose interests are threatened. They sometimes malign and spread rumours against active workers of the mandal. 'They try to poison the minds of our members against our integrity and honesty.'

Slowly, over a long period of time, they have been able to acquire the trust of their members. However, in money matters the trust is fragile. Any delay or mismanagement, their inability to give money whenever the members ask, or if they press the members for contributions for the mandal and its activities—all this tend to make the people suspicious, resistant and sometimes even hostile. The relatively well-to-do members who are not given loans remain dissatisfied and sometimes try to malign the leaders. For instance, during the inauguration of the poultry cooperative society, some villagers got drunk and started accusing the leaders of misappropriating money. They started shouting and disrupted the proceedings.

Secondly, the leaders also see a danger of internal dissension among active workers and executive committee members. The internal dissension, they feel, is likely on two grounds. One is the temptation to hold position, feel important before community members and exercise power with the local bureaucracy. Such things boost one's ego and status in the community. The other is the possibility that the executive committee members themselves may become dishonest with all the money at their disposal.

In the last year several executive committee members were changed. Among other things the president suspected two of the members of having, as he put it, 'bad intentions.'

Another difficulty that active members face is the demand on their time. With increasing activities they have to spend a lot of time in visiting government offices, preparing forms and documents and generally managing the mandal. So far they are managing with the help of even non-members, like school teachers who are supportive of their work, but it gets difficult as they take on more and more activities.

Impact

The economic activity has brought considerable relief to the poorer members of the community. Institutional lending had almost stopped as most of the villagers were not able to return loans taken from government and cooperative societies. The mandal's lending activities has bridged this gap. Had the mandal's help not come in time the incidence of land alienation would have increased, people would have had to mortgage or sell their land or ornaments and also migrate. Those who were part-time agricultural labourers would have had to become full-time labourers.

The funding by the mandal comes at the right time and without delays. Members do not have to go through procedures of filling forms, producing supportive documents, making repeated trips to taluk and district towns and bribing officials.

Economic activities have improved agricultural production. It is not clear as to how much production has increased as nobody keeps records but members talk of their production having doubled. It is certain that production has gone up since many members reported reduced borrowing from private sources and reduced migration.

Mandal leaders assert that once the poultry, milk and irrigation cooperatives get going, the economic standard of the poor in their village will definitely improve.

They also emphasize the point that because of the mandal's lending activities people have started working on their own farms. Earlier, as the poor farmers did not have necessary equipment like plough, bullock or money for inputs like seeds, fertilizers, pesticides and water, many of them would give their land for cultivation to better-off farmers and get only a share of the produce. This also made them 'lazy and form bad habits like drinking.'

More importantly, mandal leaders like to drive home the fact that borrowings by farmers from the mandal go directly into economic activities. Earlier, borrowings from the cooperatives and the government were often spent on social and religious matters. The mandal leaders see to it that the money borrowed by the member is spent on the economic activity for which it is borrowed. The mandal loans the money only after the farmer starts the work, be it well-deepening or purchasing bullocks. The mandals record in the proper use of its loans is very good.

Through social reform, social education and awareness activities, they have been successful in reducing the economic ruin of the community. They have also been successful in reducing the hold of and exploitation by the traditional leaders. Also, because of the mandal's efforts in this direction, people have started using the new services provided under the government's development programmes: immunization, attending primary health centres, sending children—both boys and girls—to school.

They have brought a great deal of information to their villages about many government programmes and schemes, procedures, rules, regulations and laws, and in general about the outside world. In doing so, they have brought to the villagers information of what is officially, and at least on paper, available to them.

Through its social action activities the mandal has educated people about exploitation, the nature of exploitation and the techniques of exploiters. Today, members of the community, even the poorest most backward and least exposed members, can tell vividly and in great detail who the exploiters are and how exactly they exploit.

Social action activities have created greater sense of partnership for the mandal and greater participation among the people. An understanding that irregular public buses, extortions by petty officials, or lack of response by their elected representatives are common community problems and can be solved by common action has developed.

The social action activities have given people the confidence that it is possible to fight powerful forces successfully. Mandal leaders say that people have become militant and now even when they go individually to government officers, they argue with them bravely and demand their due. Sometimes people take recourse to force, they stop the officials and beat them up, if the officials insult them or demand money.

Thus, it is very evident that never before in the history of village Abhlod, were the very poor and the destitute approached and catered to; was so much money and resources, so many programmes and schemes brought from outside; have so many officials and politicians visited and responded to their demands; has so much of information, knowledge, skill and confidence been developed by the poor, backward and peripheral people; as after the Abhlod Yuvak Mandal started working.

10

The Mithibor Yuvak Mandal

Mithibor village is in Chota Udepur taluk of Baroda district. It is the only group in Baroda district funded by OXFAM. Though located in Baroda district, the approach road to the village passes through Panchmahals district. Most of the interaction of the village people is with the tribals of the Devgadh Bariya taluk of Panchmahals district. This is one of the most backward villages in the tribal areas of Panchmahals and Baroda districts. In both these districts there has been considerable deforestation and there are very few patches of dense forest left. Mithibor is in the midst of one of such surviving forest land. Situated on a hill, just two kilometers away from the border of Madhya Pradesh, the village is as yet almost untouched by modernity and development. Mithibor has a population of more than 4,000 distributed in ten *falias*. The *falias* are at quite a distance from each other. Some of them are on separate hills and sometimes the distance between two *falias* is as much as four kilometers.

All the households, except five, belong to adivasis. Of the five, one belongs to a harijan who is a tailor and also a member of the mandal. There are three households of Vohra Muslims and one of a Ghanchi: all four are traders and shopkeepers.

The village has not even been covered by a cooperative society—a sector which has generally penetrated well into Gujarat's rural areas. There is an ashram school about four kilometers away. There are no other modern institutions in the village except the elected village panchayat.

The people exist on monsoon agriculture, casual and seasonal labour (for which they migrate to distant parts of the state) and by collecting forest produce and selling to the Vohra shopkeepers. The shopkeepers are known among the villagers to be the biggest cheats and exploiters. Some of the forest produce, for instance, fetch very high prices in the market, but Vohra traders buy them from the tribals against very small amounts or low quality grains, which could be as much as four to five times cheaper than the market price.

The village has only four male members, all below thirty years, who have studied up to the 7th grade. The backwardness and lack of exposure to things new and modern can be gauged from their first reaction to OXFAM support.

Genesis

OXFAM Field Officer Mistry had to visit the place several times before the people were ready to take money from an outsider. Mistry notes,

I was in touch with Narpat (Secretary of Jamran group). One evening I was talking to Narpat about finding out new contacts in the area. Narpat gave me the name of Bhaljibhai of Mithibor, who is an adivasi and had studied with Narpat in school.

I went to Mithibor next day along with Narpat to meet Bhalji-bhai. He is a CHW.[1] He has studied up to the 7th grade only. In fact in the entire village there are only four tribal youth who have studied up to the 7th. I was very keen that we should have some project in this village because the village was backward and appeared to be untouched by so-called civilized population. Besides, it seemed that exploitation by the Vohras who are running shops in the village was very high. I explained to Bhaljibhai everything about OXFAM. Narpat had also explained to him about OXFAM and about his own mandal's activities before our visit. I gave him my address and came back. The second time when I went again with Narpat to encourage Bhaljibhai to take up some project, he showed some site for lift irrigation and we requested Bhaljibhai to register the group and write to us for funds. Third time again I went to him. We saw the site and I agreed to fund. This was in the beginning of 1980. I did not hear anything from Bhaljibhai until 1983. I stopped

---

[1] Community Health Worker (CHW) now called VHG. Under the VHG scheme introduced in 1977, every village with a population of 1,000 was to have a community member selected as VHG who would provide some preliminary medicines and look after basic sanitation and hygiene of the village. He would receive Rs. 50 per month as honorarium.

going to Mithibor thinking that he and other villagers were not
interested and hence I should not go. In 1983 I heard from him
saying that he had registered the mandal with the help of the
villagers and Narpat and he requested me to visit the village.
The question before me was, why had they remained silent for
more than two years; why did they not form the mandal when I
contacted them in 1980? Interestingly, I found out that they
thought (that) I am a government officer and if they take loans
from my 'department' they will have to repay the loan and perhaps, will have to sell their lands. Also they were not very sure
about how much money they will have to spend by way of bribery
in taking this loan. But when they realised that OXFAM had
funded some of the mandals in the nearby villages of Panchmahals
district and that the villagers themselves were running the mandals
and managing the money they felt reassured and since Narpat was
in constant touch with Bhaljibhai, he advised him about the
benefits of forming a mandal in Mithibor village.

Hardly anybody from the village had ever borrowed from a
cooperative society or the government. We were repeatedly and
proudly told that 'this village is clean' (meaning nobody is under
debt to lending institutions). So the villagers of Mithibor were not
only apprehensive about Mistry's intentions but the mandal itself.
To quote Mistry again:

> We sent a cheque—the first in the village. The cheque was
> shown to all the villagers. The working committee members
> went to the bank thinking that they would get the money
> immediately. Bhaljibhai deposited the cheque at the bank. It
> took fifteen days to clear. This created a lot of misunderstand-
> ing among the members that we had simply sent, a paper which
> had no value and that '*Saheb banavi gayo*' (Saheb fooled us).
> After fifteen days when they got the money, the mandal pur-
> chased the fertilizers and when they actually started distributing
> it to the members, only then the members realised that they got
> the money and that the mandal was able to do something and
> that it was a reality.

Members and Leaders

The Mithibor mandal has only thirty-six ordinary members though it covers five villages totalling a population of more than 9,000. However, within a year of the mandal's establishment many more were willing to join. But as the mandal leaders were not sure of their intentions and since they had limited funds, the executive committee was debating about when to take them in. However, the president said that the mandal was only one year old and many procedures and norms had not been decided as yet (e.g., no membership fee was taken from the members); but once things were regularized they would admit any poor person of the village as member.

The mandal has eleven members on its executive committee. Its president is Bhaljibhai, a Rathwa tribal of twenty-four years who has studied up to the 7th grade. All other executive members are either totally illiterate or can barely write their own names. The secretary of the mandal is Narpat who is also the secretary of the Jamran village mandal. Since none of the members knew anything about keeping records or maintaining accounts they requested Narpat to become their secretary.

Bhaljibhai, the president, had also worked in a soap factory at Ahmedabad and in the railways as a casual labourer. The members of the executive committee were selected in such a way that they would represent other *falias* and villages. According to the president they had taken care to select young people and those who 'can speak' (who are vocal) and were bold enough to talk to government officials. All are small farmers (family holding being less than 7 to 8 acres and individual holding, if at all, always being less than 3 acres). They also migrate seasonally in search of labour.

In little more than one year the mandal has held about fifteen meetings. Generally there is no distinction between the executive committee meetings and general meetings. When a meeting is held whoever is interested, including a non-member, can attend and participate. Because of its many social action and protest activities, attendance is high and participation is good. In the meetings, they discuss issues related to exploitation by forest officials and traders, the activities to be taken up by the mandal, loans given by the mandal and their recovery. During our visit nearly twenty-five people had gathered. Quite a few of them participated in the discussions. Besides the president several others explained to us how the traders and money lenders cheat and exploit the villagers. They seemed to us determined, enthusiastic and confident.

According to the president, they have good support and unity in the mandal. 'But we do not have information, knowledge and experience so we do not know which activities to take up for our development.'

Funds

As mentioned earlier, the mandal had not taken any membership fee and does not have its own funds. So far the administrative expenses of registering the mandal and buying stationery etc., has been paid by Narpat whose mandal at Jamran was given some funds by OXFAM for helping other mandals. Subsequently, other minor administrative expenses have been paid by the president and some executive members out of their own pockets. The president said that they are thinking of creating their own fund through membership fees and a small levy on the loanees. This mandal had asked for only Rs. 10,000 from OXFAM. As Mistry said, 'This is the first mandal I came across which was frightened to take more money.'

Economic Activities

They distributed Rs. 9,000 out of Rs. 10,000 to all the thirty-six members to buy fertilizers. Every member was given between Rs. 200 and Rs. 400. In less than one year the mandal was able to recover Rs. 7,800 of the Rs. 9,000 lent, a remarkable recovery rate of more than 86 per cent. This is the only economic activity undertaken directly by the mandal.

Social Action

The mandal has taken up issues of exploitation by traders and the local bureaucracy, particularly the forest officials and police. Some of the examples are:

1. Four adivasis had mortgaged their land with the local Vohra trader. The land remained in the name of the adivasis but the Vohra had planted eucalyptus trees. Taking of adivasi land by non-adivasis is illegal. The mandal prepared a case and decided to file a complaint with the District Collector. However, the trader came to know about this and returned the land.

2. In case of some other adivasis of the village whose lands were mortgaged to the traders, the mandal sent a complaint to the District Collector and also informed the leader at the state level in charge of implementing the 20 point programme.[2] The Vohra traders tried to win over Bhaljibhai by offering him part of the lands but he refused. The Collector instituted an inquiry and the lands were subsequently returned.

3. A villager was illegally arrested by the police on the ground that he had killed his wife when actually she had run away. The police wanted money. The man was in police custody for nearly three weeks and was not produced in court. Bhaljibhai and a few other members of the mandal went to the taluk headquarters, met the PSI (Police Sub Inspector), threatened to start an agitation and finally got him released.

4. A forest guard had taken Rs. 1,500 from an adivasi of Mithibor village. The mandal sent a complaint along with the signature of the affected adivasi to the conservator of forests at Baroda who sent a Range Officer and forced the forest guard to return the money.

5. The newly appointed *mukhi* (village headman) was harassing the villagers and extorting money from them. The president of the mandal visited such people who had given money to the *mukhi*. He encouraged them to complain and promised the mandal's support. He helped them to write a complaint against the *mukhi* to the District Collector. At the time of this field work the Collector had promised an inquiry and scheduled a date for an officer's visit to the village in this connection.

6. The mandal asserted their political rights during the last parliamentary elections held in December 1984. In this area there is a very well-established voluntary agency working among the tribals for nearly twenty-five years. The leader of this agency is a very powerful non-tribal and once a well-known Gandhian. He is also known to be politically very powerful and with direct contact with the late Prime Minister Indira Gandhi. Reportedly he is also very close to the Vohra

---

[2] The state government has appointed a senior leader of the ruling party as president in charge of implementing the 20 Point Programme (launched nationwide by the late Prime Minister Indira Gandhi) with cabinet rank.

traders of the area and does not seem to like anybody else
working for the development of tribals in his area as it would
threaten his unquestioned control. He is apparently also
apprehensive of the activities of the Mithibor mandal. During
the parliamentary elections he had sent word through the
young Vohra deputy *sarpanch* that nobody should go to
vote. Though a Congress supporter, he was believed to be
against the official congress candidate of his constituency
and did not want him elected. He sent the message because
he knew that Mithibor village would vote for the Congress.
However, mandal leaders told the villagers to go and vote
ignoring his directive.

When the villagers of Mithibor went to the polling booth
located in the Ashramshala they were sent back by those in
charge of the polling booth saying that their votes were not
registered in that booth. Bhaljibhai immediately contacted
taluk headquarters and informed the polling officials and got
police help. Just two hours before the close of the polling
booths Mithibor villagers voted. It was the mandal who
made it possible for them to exercise their political rights
much against the wishes of a very powerful leader of a well-
established large voluntary agency.

Implications

All this has created great faith in the activities of the mandal. The
villages of Mithibor now go to the mandal about any problem they
face. Also more people now want to become members.

But this has also created problems for Bhaljibhai and some
other active leaders of the mandal. The local leaders, the *sarpanch*
of the village, the police, local forest officials are all in collusion.
The *sarpanch* does not directly harass the mandal but he does not
like their activities. He usually helps Vohra traders in exploiting
the villagers. The Vohra traders give him free grains, tea, meals
and liquor and also give him importance. The *sarpanch* has tried to
divide the mandal members several times.

The Vohra traders also tried to enlist Bhaljibhai in their game of
exploitation by offering him a part of the land they had taken from
other villagers and also by advising him that he should charge
more for the loans given by the mandal. Another young Vohra

trader who is a deputy *sarpanch* of the panchayat has also been trying to associate with Bhaljibhai by saying that he has the interests of adivasis at heart. He is trying his best to see that Bhaljibhai gives him all information about the mandal and its activities, that Bhaljibhai takes his advice and thus bring the mandal under his influence. He has formed another group and is pressurizing Bhaljibhai to merge the mandal with his group. A Vohra trader falsely implicated Bhaljibhai in a theft case. The police promptly arrested him, tied him with ropes and paraded him through the village to break his morale. However, mandal members rushed to his rescue and got him released on bail. All such incidents and the successes achieved by the mandal has brought about greater involvement of the members and unity and determination among the leaders.

Mithibor mandal is less than two years old. It has carried out very limited economic activities compared to some other groups like Gamdi and Abhlod; its leaders are neither experienced nor influential and therefore have not been able to even think of taking up other developmental activities. But the stirring and awakening that it has brought, the skills and strategies that they have learnt in fighting exploitation and the confidence and hope (as against unquestioned acceptance of the might of the dominant people) that it has raised among the community members would compare favourably with any small group or established voluntary agency which has undertaken economic or developmental activities. Taking into account the fact that Mithibor is still one of those very backward interior hilly areas where there is rampant exploitation and blatant oppression, the mandal's success and impact, in a very short period of less than two years, is remarkable.

11

The Poshina Yuvak Mandal

The New Pragati Yuvak Mandal, Poshina is situated in Poshina village of Khedbrahma taluk in Sabarkantha district. It was formed in January 1981, though it was officially registered with the Charity Commissioner in March 1982.

Poshina is a large village with a population of about 12,000 and several different castes. Although the mandal has its office in Poshina, its membership and activities are only in the neighbouring smaller villages. The mandal's activities and membership include only the weaker sections, particularly scheduled castes and scheduled tribes.

The area of tribal villages surrounding Poshina village, generally known as Poshina area, is the most backward tribal area of Sabarkantha district. Within the district it is very much in the interior and difficult to reach as only few public buses ply. The village Poshina is nearly 80 kilometers away from the district headquarter which is the main centre for all official, business and trade activities.

The dominant social groups in this area are Memon Muslims, Banias and Rajputs (locally called Darbars). All political and public institutions are dominated by these groups. Memons and Banias, besides agriculture, are involved in trade and commerce and have retail shops in the villages catering to the needs of local tribals. Rajputs are primarily landholders. All the three groups are involved in money-lending and hiring the adivasis and other low castes as labourers. They are also commonly considered exploiters of the adivasis.

In the Poshina area very little infrastructure for development has taken place. Many villages do not have proper approach roads, electricity, tap water supply and even minimal health facilities. As compared to the adivasis of Meghraj and Bhiloda taluk of Sabarkantha district the adivasis of Poshina area are socio-economically much more backward. As a result this exploitation and oppression is also severe.

The mandal's activities cover seven villages around Poshina. All these villages are 90 to 100 per cent tribal villages.

Genesis

The president of the mandal, Abdul Kureshi, a Memon Muslim, was studying in Danta town where he lived in an adivasi boarding house. While living there he came in close touch with adivasi students and learnt about their poverty and the way in which they were exploited and oppressed by the rural elite, including government personnel like the police, forest officials and revenue officials. Since then he was strongly motivated to do some social work among adivasis.

After passing his higher secondary examination he was assisting his father in the latter's retail shop in Poshina. One day he met one of his classmates from a nearby village, Lambadia. His friend informed him about a youth organization that had started in Lambadia and told him that OXFAM may give them funds to take up some economic activity if they started an organization. Kureshi talked to some other young friends in Poshina and four or five neighbouring villages. After some effort they could persuade some people to join the mandal. The mandal was formed in January 1981. However, it took them more than a year to register it with the Charity Commissioner.

At present the mandal has members from seven neighbouring villages. While it has restricted its economic activities to the seven villages its other activities like adult education is spread over several other villages. In all, the mandal has so far covered fifteen villages through its various activities.

Sometime after the mandal was formed they published a pamphlet for the agricultural labourers, informing them about the rate of minimum wages fixed by the government, telling the labourers that it was their right to demand those wages from the landlords and that they should refuse to take anything less than the minimum wages. This created a big uproar. The local leaders started inquiring what this new thing called Pragati Mandal was and how these inexperienced young people had suddenly become active and taken the initiative. The police patel and some other elites of the village threatened the mandal leaders right in the centre of town, that their houses would be burnt and they would be beaten and jailed.

Some of them tried all the way up to the state level to stop the mandal from getting registered, but they were not successful. The president of Poshina village panchayat spread the rumour that the mandal was formed to convert the adivasis into Christians. An ex-member of the Legislative Assembly and the then taluk panchayat president called the mandal leaders and asked them how come they, inexperienced young people, had formed such an organization without asking him and taking his permission and how come they had become self-appointed leaders. They replied that the mandal was legally registered; if he wanted to fight he should take up the matter legally with the mandal and not talk to them individually. The leaders stood firm against these threats and opposition and the agricultural labourers who were getting four or five rupees instead of the government-fixed rate of nine began to get seven rupees. This created a good impact and enhanced the prestige of the mandal and more people joined it in 1982.

Members and Leaders

When the mandal first started in 1981 only fifteen people agreed to become members. By the time it was registered it had twenty-one members. Soon the number had gone up to fifty-six. There are many more people in these seven villages who want to join now but the mandal has very limited funds for its loaning activity and therefore they have decided not to take more members.

Moreover, the mandal leaders feel that they do not want to emphasize their loan activity. They want to continue with it as a focal activity but wish to emphasize more its social awareness, educational and developmental activities which cover as many poor people as possible in their area. All the members belong to scheduled tribes or scheduled castes. Only the president is a Memon Muslim. The membership fee was initially Rs. 11 but was raised in 1983 to Rs. 21. This is the only mandal which regularly receives the membership fee from all its members and this is the only mandal which has raised its membership fee.

The mandal regularly holds general body meetings every four months and the Executive Committee meeting every month. The meetings are well attended and members participate actively and enthusiastically. The mandal has a norm that any member who does not attend the general body meeting three times consecutively will cease to be a member. According to the secretary four people who had become inactive were dropped from the mandal.

All important decisions are taken at the general body meetings. According to the president matters for decision are put before the general body. Discussions take place. The executive committee members have to often provide guidance because all the members are not aware of the dimensions of the issues at hand. The general body then takes a decision and a resolution is passed.

This is the only mandal that we came across which is regular in holding their meetings. They also formally pass resolutions and record them. They get their accounts audited regularly. They write periodical reports for dissemination among concerned and interested people. They have written three such reports till August 1986, one of which was published in SETU's bulletin which is widely circulated among the small groups. This is also one of the very few mandals which maintains nine different types of record books or what they call files. These files are generally regularly maintained and up to date.

The executive committee consists of eleven members. The same committee continues since its inception and even office bearers are not changed. On the change of leadership the president had the following to say in his report of the mandal for 1984:

> There has been no change in the office holders so far. We have often requested the members and brought this matter again and again before the general body meeting. But nobody is coming forward to take up this responsibility. The members have so much faith in the president, secretary and treasurer that they are certain that they (the office holders) will never do anything against the interests of the members and the mandal. Whenever we have brought up this subject of change of leadership the members do not want to even listen to it. They say, 'whoever are there are the right people for us.'

In Table 12 we give background information about the executive committee members. As the table shows, the oldest member is thirty-six years old and the youngest is nineteen years old. The

TABLE 12

Socio-Economic Background of Executive Committee Members of New Pragati Mandal, Poshina

Name	Position	Age	Occupation	Education	Own land (acres)	Family land* (acres)	Remarks
Abdul Karim Kureshi	President	21	Agriculture/ Business	SSC	4	—	—
Chunibhai B. Solanki	Secretary	20	Unemployed	SSC	—	—	Family making brooms
Manubhai Parmar	Treasurer	27	Agriculture	11th Std.	—	12	—
Maganbhai Khant	Additional Secretary	35	Agriculture	7th Std.	—	4	—
Vadabhai Parmar	Vice-President	26	Service	11th Std.	4	—	—
Chunibhai Solanki	Member	22	Agriculture	7th Std.	—	3	—
Hakmabhai Parmar	Member	35	Agriculture	8th Std.	—	4	—
Khemabhai Angari	Member	28	Agriculture	Illiterate	—	3	—
Hagrambhai Parmar	Member	35	Agriculture	5th Std.	—	4	Member of Gram Panchayat
Pravinbhai Angari	Member	19	Agriculture	7th Std.	—	4	—
Naranbhai Parmar	Member	36	Agriculture	8th Std.	—	3	—

* Family land is a joint holding owned by all the family members collectively. The member may get his share if and when it is formally divided.

president and secretary, the most active members, are twenty-one and twenty years respectively. The average age of the executive committee is 27.6 years. Thus the leadership is quite young.

Of the eleven executive committee members, the president is a Muslim, the secretary and another member belong to the scheduled castes, while the remaining eight members all belong to the scheduled tribes. The peculiarity of this group is that the president is a Muslim, the treasurer is a tribal and the secretary belongs to scheduled caste. Yet all the three are known to be working as a solid, strong team. The mandal has only four executive members educated up to high school level, while the rest of the eleven members are educated up to the primary level or below. There is only one member who is doing a very low level job. The president owns four acres of agricultural land and shares a small general retail shop with his father. Others are small landholders. Nine out of the eleven members have three to four acres of land which is jointly owned with other family members. Thus the leadership of this mandal is from the weaker section, young, poor and not highly educated.

Funding

OXFAM had given approximately Rs. 28,000 towards economic and social awareness activities till 1984. Besides, a small amount of Rs. 1,500 was also given for administrative expenses. In 1985 the mandal received Rs. 18,600 for adult education from OXFAM. The mandal also receives a Rs. 3,000 yearly grant from the Prohibition Department of the government to run a cultural centre for propagation against drinking liquor. Except the very small membership fee the mandal has no other income or fund of its own.

Activities

The mandal carries out economic and social awareness and social justice activities. Among the economic activities the mandal gives loans from its OXFAM funds for making brooms, for fertilizers and pesticides and for deepening wells. Till 1985, the mandal has given loans to five scheduled caste members for broom-making, thirty-three members for fertilizers and pesticides and thirty-one members for deepening of wells. These loans have in some cases, depending on recovery, been given two or three times.

The mandal does not stop at merely distributing loans. It helps its members in making the best use of the loans. For instance, in case of loans given for making brooms the mandal helped the loanees to get the raw materials and organized the sales of the brooms so that the members would get the maximum price. Similarly, for fertilizers and pesticides, the lenders themselves went to the sales depot, contacted the concerned persons and remained present while the loanees actually bought the fertilizers. That way the members did not have to spend time in going repeatedly to the sales depot and they got good quality materials at a fixed rate. This also ensured that the members would use the loan money for the purpose for which the loans were given. The decision for giving loans is taken very carefully. Members are asked to apply. The merits of the applications are considered by the committee. Each applicant is visited by the committee members at his own residence.

In case of loans for deepening wells the committee examined each well and in some cases even climbed down the well. The committee members helped to rent the necessary equipment for deepening the well, insisted that family members of the loanee provide the labour and often remained present while the well-deepening work was being carried out.

The recovery rate of the mandal is very good. In the first year they had 100 per cent recovery. In 1983 their recovery rate was not good because that year crops, particularly cotton, were spoiled because of excessive cold. Even then they repeatedly moved from village to village and explained to the people that if they did not return at least a part of the due instalment the group will break up. Many members, even when they were in severe hardship financially, paid back part of the due instalment to show that they wanted the mandal to remain active and strong. The mandal's recovery rate is between 70 per cent during a bad year to 100 per cent in a good year.

The mandal's major thrust is however not so much on economic activities as on social action and social awareness activities. The major method that they use is to organize gettogethers of people—both members and non-members—under one pretext or another and give information, generate debates and discussions.

As mentioned earlier this is one mandal which holds executive committee and general body meetings frequently and regularly.

After its registration in March 1982 till January 1984 it had held fifteen executive committee meetings and five general body meetings. At these meetings, besides the mandal's economic activities discussion about the need to strengthen the mandal, for unity among the poor, exploitation of the poor, the weaknesses of the poor people and such issues are continuously discussed. Whatever difficulties the mandal leaders face, particularly from outsiders, such as threats or harassment or attempts to tempt and corrupt them, are brought out into the open at these meetings and discussed.

In 1983–84 the mandal contacted and influenced the district adult education department to start fifteen adult education classes in the Poshina area. They also searched and identified 'young good men' as instructors for some of these classes. And while the mandal's role, here, was only that of a facilitator they used their contact and influence with the village people to have adults attend these classes regularly.

In 1984–85, through the Nehru Youth Centre[1] of the Sabarkantha district the mandal itself started and organized fifteen adult education classes.

In 1985–86, with an OXFAM support of Rs. 18,600, the mandal started ten adult education classes. For these classes, they organized intensive training programmes for the ten adult education instructors, with the help of the Nehru Youth Centre. In the adult education classes run by the mandal they make particular efforts to see that the attendance is high and regular. Women's classes are also run. Besides literacy and numeracy, great deal of emphasis is given to information about health, education and development programmes. Information is given and discussions are held, on approaching government officials for one's and the community's needs, on cleanliness and hygiene, on alcoholism, on bad social customs, on giving education to all children, on exploitation and oppression of the poor, on the value of one's vote, on the benefits of unity and organization, on forming youth organizations and many other social and political issues. The objective of the mandal is to use these classes as a vehicle for social awareness, conscientization and mobilization and organization of the tribals of the Poshina area.

---

[1] This is a government organization established to carry out cultural and educational activities among the youth.

Besides adult education classes the mandal has organized *shibirs* on various subjects. Between June 1983 and March 1986 the mandal organized ten *shibirs*: of landless labour, youth leadership, tribal development and women. The mandal has also hosted a *shibir* of similar youth organizations of Sabarkantha district.

In the women's *shibir* they took up questions related to women. According to the president:

> Adivasi women of this area are very backward. Very few are literate. They are oppressed by various kinds of customs including polygamy. If a married woman is found talking to some man, fights and murders take place. The whole process of revenge and counter revenge starts and the tribals get ruined in the debts they incur in these quarrels. Our women's *shibir* helped a great deal in bringing these issues into the open. In fact, in our memory, the women of this area got together for the first time in such numbers for a non-social and non-religious activity like a *shibir*.

Outsiders like government officials, social workers and activists also attend these *shibirs* and that way they also come to know the mandal and its activities.

Because of the contacts that the mandal has developed with some established organizations, like the Nehru Youth Organization, the exposure of the members and even non-members to the outside world has increased. The Nehru Youth Organization for instance has sent some of the young people of this area, including a dance troupe, to the various cultural and sports gatherings in other parts of the state and the country. They have also started participating in larger issues and organizations though yet in a limited way. The mandal is participating actively in the Forest Workers' Union of Sabarkantha District started by Mistry, OXFAM's ex-field officer. The president of the mandal is the president of the Forest Workers' Union. The mandal organized a large meeting of the people of Poshina area to oppose the 1982 Forest Policy Bill of the Government of India.

Difficulties and Limitations

The Poshina mandal now is active and cohesive but initially it faced many difficulties. Firstly, Poshina as already mentioned, is a very backward tribal area. To initiate any non-religious, non-social activity and organization where poor tribals themselves would be involved was a difficult proposition. The present president of Poshina mandal and his two or three friends had to struggle hard and put in a lot of leg work in order to persuade the people. It took them more than a year to persuade thirty people to become members and register the mandal.

Secondly, they faced considerable opposition from the entrenched vested interests of their area. In the beginning some Patel landlords along with the local politicians threatened the three pioneers of the mandal. They threatened to beat them up, burn their houses and put them into jail. When this did not discourage them attempts were made to tempt and lure them away. They were asked to join the youth Congress-I and were assured positions of leadership in local organizations in future if they gave up the mandal. Next, rumours were spread against the leaders that they were motivated by self-interest in running the mandal and giving loans; that they were trying to convert the adivasis into Christians. People were also being warned that they might get into some legal trap by taking loans from the mandal. Attempts were also made to corrupt them. In the 1984 report the President noted that, 'the *Ujaliat Varg* (upper class) approach them and suggest that mandal leaders should give them an interest-free loan of Rs. 2,000 in the name of some adivasi and they would give the leaders a "cut".' These vested interests have now given up any active harassment. According to the President 'on the surface they keep good relations but they would strike against the mandal if they got the chance.'

Thirdly, because of the poverty in the area, the mandal has not been able to generate its own funds. This situation is really not different from any other mandal. In fact this is one of the few mandals which gets its membership fees and the small five per cent surplus it charges on the loans, regularly. Yet the mandal is not financially self-sufficient; nor does it appear to be headed in that direction. The mandal leaders are aware of it. They, in fact, feel that they should concentrate more and more on mobilizational and social awareness activities. But they do need some economic activities as a focal point to keep the mandal going. Also because of the limited funds for their economic activities they cannot increase the membership though many more people want to join now.

Finally, in spite of the fact that this mandal is systematically managed and very active it has not been successful to any considerable extent in bringing the benefits of development programmes of the government to their area. In fact the interaction of the mandal with taluk and district level development bureaucracy is very limited while linkages with taluk and district level political leaders is absent.

While it has close contacts with the Nehru Youth Centre and the prohibition department none of these two benefit them in terms of economic development or infrastructure for development activities. The Tribal Sub-plan Administration, a government agency which is of most direct relevance to them is not even aware of the mandal's existence. This is so because the area is very backward. Unlike some other mandals, like Gamdi or Abhlod in Panchmahals or Isri-Kundol or Mota Kantharia in other parts of Sabarkantha district, the Poshina mandal has no leader in government service to help them build their network of contacts. Poshina area being backward there are very few local tribals in government and politics.

Though this could be a blessing in disguise as far as the mandal is concerned. Mandals which get involved in bringing benefits of development programmes also get involved in manipulations and compromises with the local administration and politicians. They spend a lot of time and energy in this. The efforts and orientations of leaders of these mandals seem to get diverted to management of development and they seem to undermine mobilizational, participatory and social action aspects of their mandal's activities. In fact, unconsciously and gradually, the very idea of the mandal seems to get undermined in favour of starting and managing new development oriented activities and organizations. In spite of more than four years' of its existence Poshina has remained quite active in social action and mobilization work.

Impact

Poshina's economic activities have brought considerable relief. Most members report that their agricultural production have gone up considerably. But more importantly, they have experienced considerable relief from exploitation. When they used to do transactions individually they were cheated and exploited at every step. They had to borrow money at as heavy a rate of interest as 110 per cent from landlords, money-lenders and traders. They had to face considerable harassment. All this has now reduced considerably.

As the mandal reported in its 1986 report of activities:

> On one side the income of the capitalists has been reduced, on the other side the exploitation of the poor has stopped. Thirdly, our mandal which was dormant in the first year has become active. Another major benefit is that many adivasi men used to mortgage their land and their women's ornaments which has also now decreased.

Because of the educational, social awareness and social action activities the mandal feels that it has achieved much. 'Because of these activities,' writes the president in his 1986 annual report, 'the mandal's span and coverage has become wider, it has become a better known organization, positive attitudes towards the mandal has strengthened it and we have become enthusiastic about taking up new activities.'

By organizing social awareness *shibirs* the mandal has had considerable impact in bringing about a sense of brotherhood and unity among adivasis. As mentioned earlier, in this area quarrels and even pitched battles among adivasis take place particularly on disputes relating to women. These result in injuries, killings and enmity among different groups of adivasis. Taking and paying of revenge money (amounts ranging between Rs. 10,000 and 45,000) also push them deep into debt. 'In our *shibirs* adivasis from different villages come, they sit, talk, eat and stay together. We discuss these matters openly. This has helped to reduce quarrels and fights and the sense of brotherhood has increased.'

Adivasis have also become more aware of exploitation and how the exploiters try to cheat and divide them. Because of the mandal's activities against drinking of liquor many adivasis in the area have given up drinking.

In two villages of this area—Chandran and Dantia—the mandal has helped to start and register two new youth organizations.

By holding a *shibir* exclusively for women and by laying more emphasis on women in their adult education classes they have also started the work of women's awareness. 'They have started coming out of their homes and begun talking.'

On the whole, in a very backward and remote tribal area of Poshina the New Pragati Yuvak Mandal, in less than five years, with less than Rs. 30,000 rupees, working with a small team of young men from the poorest and lowest strata of society with only primary or secondary education, has had considerable and extensive impact.

12

Micro Action and Macro Issues

If the phenomenon of small action groups of weaker sections is to be viewed as a conventional local development effort, in which many established voluntary organizations are involved, then these mandals are performing well.

Their economic development activities are very limited. These activities have not and will not raise the standard of living of the poor to whom they give very small amounts of funds. These activities are adhoc in the sense that they respond to immediate needs and are not planned to take care of economic problems of the poor in a permanent way. On the other hand the economic activities have brought various types of relief to the very poor. It has given them relief from the clutches of landlords, money-lenders and traders who are the traditional exploiters; and *sarpanches* and leaders of cooperative societies who are the new exploiters. This is something which established voluntary agencies have achieved with difficulty, with a larger resource base and over a long period of time. However, it is clear that the economic activities of these groups cannot make any significant impact on the patterns of economic relationships and the economic structure of these backward areas. The issue is important because if these groups cannot make that kind of impact, their small relief-type economic activities will not take them very far. Shortage of funds, problems of recovery, pilferage, corruption, dissension over management and distribution of funds and primarily the inadequacy of their economic operation would sooner or later overwhelm them. As a starting point their operation is very effective but it cannot continue to remain there.

To some, particularly those who take the management of development approach, it is a question of taking the benefits of development to the poor. Since governments and macro public institutions have not been successful in doing so, the poor have to be prepared and strengthened to reach up and pull down the benefits of development. These groups could be a first step in moving from voluntary efforts by outsiders to efforts by insiders themselves to develop themselves. After all, in the ultimate sense of development, people themselves should look after their own development.

In this respect these groups have done quite well keeping in mind the fact that they started with severe handicaps. When they began they had hardly any information, skills, experience or confidence. They had meagre resources. Simple things like raising the bus fare to go to the taluk office were major hurdles. It was also a problem to obtain an audience with officials for such ill-educated, ill-clothed people. In their initial encounters with local officials some leaders suffered from acute nervousness and could hardly open their mouths. As the president of the Mithibor mandal said, 'we wanted such people (in our mandal) who could speak.' Then there was also the problem of local bureaucracy recognizing such groups. Bureaucracy was more accustomed to conventional local organizations like panchayats and cooperatives. Organizations of the people running on their own do not fit into the bureaucratic scheme of things. Starting from this situation, slowly and with perseverence, they have increased their access to bureaucracy very substantially. As we have seen they have brought many benefits to their people from different development programmes and schemes. By relentlessly pursuing the administration they have made local officials visit their communities more often. They have made the petty government functionary more responsive by constant watch and vigilance.

For those who profess self-reliance in the development process by developing skills, confidence and participation of the poor, these Yuvak Mandals provide a good model. We have stated that these groups are unusual in that they are entirely manned and managed by the community people themselves. Except the small amounts of funds from OXFAM and periodic brief visits by the field officer, the groups had to fend for themselves in every way. Right from learning how to register their groups they had to plan and manage economic and other developmental activities, had to learn to deal with bureaucracy. politics and established voluntary organizations. They had to confront bureaucracy and fight against corruption and organize protests; they had to contend with traditional leaders of their own tribes and entrenched interests in their villages.

In a short time of less than four years they have generated considerable involvement and participation of the poor and the dominated people. The variety and degree of participation and involvement generated by these groups of the illiterate, poor and peripheral people, through developmental and economic activities, dialogues, *shibirs*, meetings, satyagrahas, protests and so forth, is indeed unprecedented. By very conservative estimates and only considering the thirty-eight groups covered in this study, their activities have in one way or another touched nearly 80,000 people of about fifty villages and have at one time or another generated active involvement of several hundred people.

In our discussion on the groups and their interaction with the outside world, we have mentioned that there are some missionary and Gandhian/Sarvodaya type of organizations working in these areas. Some of these organizations have been working for three decades or more. They are managed by strong and resourceful people and have not suffered from the kind of handicaps that these groups have. And yet, they are rarely known to have generated this extent and level of participation of the marginalized people.

If development is a question of mainstreaming the peripheral and marginalized people, then the work of these groups is bringing them into the social, economic, political and even cultural (which some may not approve) mainstream, within the limits of their resources, circumstances and perceptions.

OXFAM has spent Rs. 1.3 million over a period of four years on fifty-three such groups in Gujarat. It is eleven per cent of its total budget for the Western Indian region in the four year period (See Appendix II). If one keeps in mind this small resource input and the severe handicaps with which these mandals had started their work, their performance is indeed remarkable considering the variety of their activities and the extent of their coverage.

But can one therefore profess that this is the mode and model of development to be followed in the country? At a more practical level one may ask about the chances of sustaining the groups and the processes that they have generated. The questions of longevity and replicability are inevitably and repeatedly asked. But implied is the more complex question of the potentiality and possibility of these small action groups as one more among many such micro movements which are engaged in alternative development that would eventually lead to a just and equalitarian social order.

Simply and bluntly put: would these groups survive, multiply and aggregate, so that along with other types of micro movements they accomplish what government and its administrative machinery, state and its political institutions have not been able? Do these groups have, as some observers of micro movements have stated, the capacity to grow quantitatively and 'blossom into a macro movement for alternative development?'

Those who see in micro actions of various types a possibility of alternative political process and alternative development that would bring about a new social and political order, need to take a close and more realistic look.

All the macro attempts to change the social order in the last forty years, from within the official system (community development and panchayati raj, the micro and bottom up planning, poverty alleviation and other development programmes and schemes), outside the system (Bhoodan and JP movements) and against the system (the Naxalite movement), have failed. In that context these micro movements are indeed worth looking at; but in the absence of a concrete alternative model, whether these small efforts would eventually lead to a fundamental social transformation is debatable.

There is now enough experience to show that voluntary local efforts, either of the developmental type or mobilizational-struggle type, run into serious problems after an impressive initial innings. Many established voluntary organizations and successful movements, after the first ten or fifteen years, have either stagnated or disintegrated.

Compromises and adjustments required for funds and facilities, onslaught of external forces, internal dissension in the organizations or communities have led to serious problems. Some who showed impressive achievements in the activities they had taken up at the local level but did not see any basic or lasting changes taking place, moved from one activity to another, from one area to another, and from being independent of the government to collaborating with it. Some felt that after their achievement in their local areas they had to extend and expand in order to make an impact. So they got into committees, conferences and consultancies. In the process they began to loose credibility with their communities, other activists, and sometimes the second cadre of workers in their own organizations.

Exhaustion, frustration and cynicism in their attitudes; and distortions and even corruption in their modus operandi have sometimes crept in. Often this stagnation or disintegration is ascribed to managerial factors. Lack of planning and strategy, overfunding, rapid expansion, lack of skilled and committed workers, overbearing leadership not allowing a second level of leadership to develop, are some of the commonly mentioned factors in evaluation.

But it is worth probing whether this stagnation, decay or disintegration is also due to absence of a concrete macro alternative with which these local initiatives can be linked and aggregated. Having successfully worked at local levels, 'what next?' is a nagging question that though not explicitly articulated often seems to be a major cause of stagnation, distortion and disintegration of these more established organizations and better known movements. In spite of noteworthy achievements in developmental activities and in fighting against local corruption and exploitation, it is clear that small action groups cannot make any dent on the nature of administrative and political systems of even their own taluk, far from having any impact on the larger socio-economic structure. It is very likely that these groups, like the more established organizations and movements, would with time get frustrated, exhausted, coopted or corrupted.

Are they expected to be in a perpetual state of mobilization, organization and participation? There is no reason to assume that the process of awareness, conscientization and participation will be incremental and aggregative all the time.

Earlier we had observed that members and leaders of these groups have no faith in politics, politicians and parties. They see politicians as corrupt, power hungry, selfish people and politics as dirty. And yet they go to local politicians for solving their problems and also support and campaign for them in the elections. Some of the leaders of these groups themselves have contested elections in villages, taluk and district panchayat bodies. Their modus operandi is similar to any conventional politician when they try to get the candidacy from any political party for the elections. They see no other alternative.

In one of the training programmes I was discussing the issues of fundamental structural change and going beyond local developmental activities. A leader of one of the small groups asked, 'Has not all this been given by our constitution; is there anything in our constitution that we need to change? What is it that we are supposed to do for this fundamental change?' One may elaborate and specify on this question. If our political parties, our electoral processes, our representative institutions and our public administration cannot deliver the goods, what other institutional alternatives do we need?

In our *shibirs* for these groups we raise the issues of the unjust and exploitative social, economic and political system. But when it comes to discussing alternatives, the new social order and its structure, the alternative economic arrangements, the new political system and its institutions, we falter. We talk vaguely of struggle, conscientization and consciousness, mobilization and participation.

The higher order activists and intellectuals have somehow not bothered to develop political techniques nor evolve an alternative political model towards which these small groups can direct their micro efforts. Of course, one can argue as sometimes the higher order activists and intellectuals do, that these micro efforts will (somehow) lead to macro alternatives. Who are we to impose a model; no blue-print should be given; people themselves will evolve it.

The stronger, more competent and developmentally more successful groups like Gamdi, Abhlod or Chunakhan have perhaps felt both the hollowness of such postures and the chasm between their work at local levels and the macro issues of national and global forces as being the cause of their poverty and suffering. Like seasoned politicians these groups and their leaders are not only beginning to manipulate politics and administration but even outside activists and intervenors.

Appendix II

Note on the OXFAM Effort in Small Group Development

This note was written as part of the report prepared for SETU and OXFAM for circulation among concerned people. Since it would be of interest to many activists, voluntary organizations and funding agencies it is reproduced here. What is reproduced here is what was written in early 1985. Since then I have 'heard' that there have been many changes in the OXFAM (Western Region) office, its funding patterns and its approach to supporting small groups of weaker sections.

In 1979, OXFAM (Western Region) decided to shift its emphasis from larger established voluntary agencies to small village level groups of weaker sections of society. The focus was on backward areas and weaker sections: Dharampur taluk of Valsad district, Panchmahals and Sabarkantha districts and tribals, scheduled castes and other backward castes. By the middle of 1984 OXFAM had funded fifty-three such groups in Gujarat and eight groups in Rajasthan of tribals, scheduled castes and other backward classes.

This approach is unusual if not unique in two respects: (*a*) to the best of my knowledge I do not know of any other region in the country where so many small groups[1] have been formed. These are entirely manned and managed by weaker sections themselves without any sustained intervention or continuous presence of an outsider; (*b*) no other foreign funding agency has a direct and sustained involvement in small groups of weaker sections at the lowest level—the village. It would be, therefore, useful to know more about this approach and how it is actually practiced.

---

[1] At the last count the number of such small groups is nearly 200, though all of them are not funded by OXFAM.

OXFAM Set-Up

The OXFAM set-up in the region consists of two field staff[2] and an administrative assistant. One of the two field staff is a Field Director, who is also the office head. The field officer is the one who is primarily involved in field level activities. He is involved in all the work regarding small groups in the whole region as also all other activities of OXFAM. The region covers two states of Rajasthan and Gujarat. There is thus primarily one person from OXFAM looking after the work of the small groups spread over the eastern belt of Gujarat and some areas of Rajasthan state. Till June 1984, part of the ground floor of the Field Director's residence was used as the OXFAM Office.[3]

Identification of Individuals and Groups

Once it was decided to fund small groups directly, the concentration was on two districts: Panchmahals and Sabarkantha. Later on Dharampur, the most backward and almost entirely tribal taluk of Valsad district, was also included. Even in these two districts only the tribal and backward taluks were included. While generally attention was directed towards selected districts there was no rigidity about it. If potentialities or need was seen in some other area then people were encouraged to form groups and support was given. Thus, two groups in a forward district of Ahmedabad and one group in Baroda district were also supported.[4]

Madhusudan Mistry, a Field Officer, who had joined OXFAM in 1979 was the person who is involved in this work from OXFAM.[5] His method was to meet the established voluntary agencies, government officials of his acquaintance or any person who could give some information about any group or individual at the village level. A voluntary agency, for instance, put him in touch with the president of the Isri-Kundol group who had already

---

[2] In April 1984, OXFAM added another female field officer. Since 1985, several other additions have taken place.

[3] Now OXFAM has a full fledged separate office.

[4] OXFAM has also supported four groups in Banaskantha district besides some cooperative societies.

[5] He left OXFAM by the end of 1985 to start his own voluntary agency called DISHA. The author is associated with it as a trustee.

formed a mandal which was giving loans to two or three individuals from its very meagre resources created by very small contributions from a few persons. After contacting the president and getting more information about him and his group, talking to other community members, considering the need and potentiality of taking up new activities and so on, it was decided to give funds to this group. Once this group started its activities, people from nearby villages were also encouraged to form groups. Later on Isri-Kundol became a core group which helped in forming nearly ten such groups in the nearby villages.

Once when Mistry was going on one of his many field trips on a motorbike, he saw a signboard on the highway on which the name of a mandal was written. He stopped, went into the village by the side of the highway and made inquiries. He found that a small number of adivasis had already formed a group and was running a nursery school. He talked to them about OXFAM and after a couple more visits, the Adivasi Pragati Mandal of Navavenpur in Bhiloda taluk was funded.

In case of the Zalod group, Mistry was informed about its activities by one of his contacts. Mistry went to Zalod and met its president with whom he discussed the socio-economic problems of the area. He suggested to the president that he organize a *shibir* for adivasis from the surrounding areas. A training camp was organized in which about forty women and fifty men participated. This training camp was funded by OXFAM. In the case of this group the funding was first for a training camp and only later was the group given funds for its activities. Sometimes, the members of a village who hear about the activities of another group approach OXFAM for help in forming such a group and for funds.

When Mistry felt that an area was very backward and that a group activity would help the people, he put in considerable effort to see that a group was formed. Thus, the formation of the Mithibor group required considerable effort and persuasion both by Mistry and the contact person as the people of Mithibor were afraid of taking money from anybody. The first visit of Mistry to this mandal was in 1980. It took nearly three years for the mandal to get registered.[6]

---

[6] See Chapter 10 which describes in Mistry's own words the process of the formation of Mithibor group.

OXFAM Funding

Tables 13 and 14 present data about OXFAM funding. In about four and a half years, OXFAM has funded fifty-three small groups to the tune of Rs. 1.37 million. In Panchmahals little more than half a million rupees have been distributed among twenty groups, while in Sabarkantha almost an equal amount has been distributed among sixteen groups (Table 14). The proportion of OXFAM funding to small groups out of its total budget for the region has ranged from 6 per cent to 17 per cent only, though small groups have become its major activity in the region since 1980 (Table 13).

TABLE 13
**Proportion of OXFAM Funding to Small Groups
out of its Total Budget for the Region**

Year	Total Budget (Rs)	Funding to Small Groups (Rs)	Proportion of small groups funding of total budget (per cent)
1980	2,799,360	200,790	7.1
1981	2,439,784	395,730	16.2
1982	3,004,111	525,159	17.4
1983	3,978,023	257,048	6.4
Total	12,221,278	1,378,727	11.2

Note: These figures are for OXFAM's Western Region as a whole which includes Rajasthan.

TABLE 14
**OXFAM Funding to Small Groups in Various Districts
of Gujarat during the Period 1980–1984**

District	Amount (Rs)	No. of Groups
Valsad (Dharampur Taluk only)	139,200	9
Baroda (Mithibor only)	11,500	1
Panchmahals	560,650	24
Ahmedabad	88,000	3
Sabarkantha	560,712	16
Total	1,360,062	53

It may also be noted that its funding to the small groups in the year 1983 has been the lowest, 6 per cent only. OXFAM funding patterns, like everything about its activities in regard to the small groups, are highly variable and geared to individual situations. Some notable features of OXFAM funding are:

1. OXFAM has not taken a programmatic approach where it gives priority to a particular programme of development and then give loans to only those who are already doing or willing to take up that particular activity.
2. The total amount of funding per group is very small. Funding to different groups varies in amounts from as low as Rs. 10,000 per group to as high as Rs. 70,000.
3. There is no fixed periodical input to each group. Some groups like Zalod have been given the money at six different times (as many as three times in one year), while groups like Chitadara have received funds only once in four years.
4. Groups are given loans repayable to OXFAM in instalments after a fixed period. There are also revolving funds which are not to be returned to OXFAM; and grants for specific short-term activities.
5. Groups have been given funds mainly for economic activities, but sometimes developmental activities like balwadis have also been funded. In a few cases groups were given grants for what are called administrative expenses. These are generally given for meeting the travel, stationery and contingent expenses of groups who are helping other communities to form groups, with accounts or registration, etc.

The amount and the type of funds, as also the activities for which funds are to be given, are all decided on the basis of the assessment of needs, circumstances of a particular group, commitment and integrity of the leaders and the record of the group in managing its affairs. The assessment is done by the field officer along with leaders and members of the group. At the first instance, the groups are asked to come up with the type of activity they would like to undertake and the amount of funds required. Following a discussion with them, the activity and amount are decided. Sometimes it takes more than one visit by the field officer to the concerned village and two or three rounds of discussions. Village people also visit the OXFAM office for such discussions. Sometimes groups have been given funds immediately after their registration, sometimes funds are given only after they have taken up and managed some activities and sometimes no funds are given at all, though Mistry may keep in touch with such non-funded groups and help them in other ways. Funding has also depended upon need and opportunity. For instance, Margala group has been given funds to repair and deepen a well owned by an individual, with an agreement to give water to other members of the group. That perhaps was the only opportunity to generate any activity in that community.

In Jamran, the first funding was to a village panchayat and not to an independent group. Jamran group was funded later when the people of Jamran came to know about OXFAM because of the fund given to the village panchayat. In Mistry's own words:

I was in search of contact and was going round villages and institutions to find out people who were involved in social work. This was in 1979 immediately after I joined OXFAM. Just for curiosity (during one of the trips) I stopped at village Sagatala where the gram panchayat is housed. I entered the room and met Punjabhai Patel, the *sarpanch*, who thought that I was a (labour) contractor and had gone there in search of labourers. I told him about OXFAM and the purpose of my visit. It was he who took me to Jamran village to show the well on which the Jamran *sarpanch* had prepared a scheme to irrigate 30 acres of land. Due to conflict between two engineers on the amount of water in the well, the scheme was not sanctioned by the government. I saw the well and the land and met the people. I could not meet Masoorbhai, the *sarpanch*, who was out of the village. I left my address and a message for Masoorbhai to contact me. Masoorbhai wrote me letters afterwards. I was again in Jamran but could not meet Masoorbhai. Masoorbhai came twice to Ahmedabad but could not locate the OXFAM Office. I was fortunately able to locate him in Jamran on my fifth visit to that village and we decided that OXFAM would give some grant for a diesel pump-set to irrigate the village. But the question was whom to fund. We found out that we can make a grant to the gram panchayat. This is how we made our first grant to a gram panchayat.

Later on, Masoorbhai's friend Narpat formed a mandal in Jamran which was funded by OXFAM.

Narpat, the leader of the Jamran group had inspired Laxman-bhai to form a group in Lavaria village. Lavaria group was funded not so much because the economic activity it proposed was worth funding, rather because its leader was a very committed person. He approached OXFAM only after registering the group. He had fought single-handedly against the corruption of the village *sar-panch* and the taluk development officer. It was, therefore, felt that a mandal would provide a good base for Laxmanbhai, its president, to mobilize people for social action activities.

These then are some of the ways by which OXFAM made decisions for funding small groups. OXFAM funding to small groups is an excellent example of situational flexibility. It has responded to needs and circumstances without any standardization or preconceived notions about types of activities, forms of organ-izations, amounts, periodicity or conditions of funding.

Monitoring and Intervention

As has been repeatedly mentioned earlier, the groups take their own decisions about the type of activities and the mode of doing these activities. The entire management is by the group leaders. In all this, OXFAM's intervention is minimum. When groups come up with a request for funding a particular activity, its viability and need are assessed and at that time Mistry may suggest alternatives, but that is the point at which there may be any major intervention. Even at such time the intervention is in the form of a dialogue and discussion, such that it helps the group leaders to realize the implications of their proposals. Sometimes Mistry gives them information about the new programmes, rules and regulations. For instance, in Mithibor, he found that many tribals had mort-gaged their land with the local Muslim traders. He advised the president to prepare a list and send it to the district collector along with a copy to the state level leader in charge of the 20 Point Programme. However, even in this kind of advice and suggestion, only minimum inputs are given. The field officer does not go to government offices on behalf of groups, nor does he carry out their work. It is they who have to collect information, make applica-tions, pay visits and deal with outsiders.

When absolutely necessary OXFAM has facilitated some help from outside. This is mostly done indirectly, that is by funding some other agency or individual to go and help the concerned groups. But in rare situations OXFAM has directly undertaken to provide such help. For instance, OXFAM once appointed a person to advise the groups about agriculture. Such direct help is given on technical or specific administrative matters only. We have already mentioned that some of the more experienced groups were identified as core groups, to help the new groups with accounts, records and books. In Dharampur, one person is appointed to help the groups with accounts, records and other activities. Dharampur groups are highly inexperienced and the leaders are not educated enough to keep accounts and records. The person is not appointed directly by OXFAM.

Monitoring of the mandals is not structured and standardized. Mistry visits the groups frequently. Normally he travels for about fifteen days in a month to these villages. During his visits he meets leaders, members and sometimes people of the village. Overnight stays are generally in the villages so that the time at night is also used for discussion. Mistry discusses with the group significant aspects of their activities. Or the groups raise matters of their immediate preoccupations. He also looks at their records, makes assessments of the amount of loan given to members, its use, its benefits (like increase in production) and recovery.

Mistry has established very good rapport with the groups. He is very friendly with the groups and the leaders tell him virtually everything: about their activities; their experiences with administrators, politicians and traders; incidents and events in their community or in other groups; and their personnel problems (which sometimes have serious implications for the mandals). On the other hand he is uncompromising, unrelenting and very tough when required; particularly when it is a matter of recovery of loans, mismanagement or misappropriation of money. At times he has gone to the banks to verify whether the amount reported to have been deposited was actually in the balance or not. In the case of the leader of a women's group who had used the mandal's money for her personal work, Mistry relentlessly followed the matter till she sold her ornaments and repaid the money to the mandal.

Here is another case which gives an idea of how relentlessly such matters are pursued. In the case of Chhitadara Yuvak Mandal, Mistry on his visit to the village found that the members had repaid their loans but the money was not returned by the group leaders to OXFAM. Mistry suspected that the president and secretary had misappropriated the money. Since the president and secretary do not live in Chhitadara village, Mistry took with him two members of the mandal and went to the president's house 18 kilometers away from Chhitadara. The president said that the money was with the secretary who lived in Modasa, a taluk town nearby. So Mistry went there. On reaching Modasa they found that the secretary had gone to his in-law's house in another village. So the same night they went to the secretary's in-law's village and halted there for the night. Next day the party along with the secretary came back to Chhitadara village. Since the secretary had no ready money with him he was asked to issue a post-dated cheque on the condition that he would deposit the money before the cheque was due.

There is, however, no standard and structured device of monitoring nor any fixed periodical monitoring. Groups are supposed to get their accounts audited and submit such audited accounts to the Charity Commissioner as well as to OXFAM. Not all groups are prompt. But since this is a legal requirement sooner or later they must comply. Mistry had also devised a sort of format in which he filled-up various types of information on groups during his visits. Some groups were asked to send information along the lines of the format. So far it has been filled up only once. Since it is not even printed, information is not gathered on all points for all mandals. Moreover, some mandals have not supplied this information at all.

This informal and non-structured way of monitoring has so far worked well because Mistry has all the information about the groups at his fingertips. However, as the number of groups increase and the area of coverage widens this informal and ad hoc method will not suffice.

Already, Mistry's visits per group in the last year have become less frequent because of their growing numbers. Therefore, now he has to select and concentrate on problem groups.

What is unusual about OXFAM's approach is the freedom and flexibility and avoidance of standardization and uniformity. This is reflected in the quantity of funds given, specific times at which they are given, types and periodicity of funds, identification and selection of groups in monitoring and intervention. Every decision is tailored to each individual situation. It is in this very specific sense, a 'need-based' approach.

I have made observations and suggestions at appropriate places in the text. I have discussed the activity-based implications and impact of the groups in the chapters on activities, and the implications and possibilities of this small group phenomenon in relation to wider issues in the last chapter. I shall not repeat them here. But I note here some general observations which may be of interest to OXFAM and to other funding agencies as well as activists and action groups.

1. In my opinion, the phenomenon of small action groups of weaker sections is a noteworthy success given any criterion of change or development: economic benefits and relief to the poor; reaching of development activities to the poor; awareness; conscientization; mobilization; organization; social action for justice; development of skills, competence, confidence and self-reliance among weaker, down-trodden and very poor people; and in general empowerment of the community. I have not come across any effort, voluntary or governmental, which has made such an impact on so many poor people, with such meagre financial input (Rs. 1.36 million), in such a short time (about four years) and such limited intervention (one and half person assuming that the field director spent at least half of his time on this activity).

2. In spite of some mismanagement, or misappropriation of funds by groups that we have discussed, I have not seen a financial input by any agency, least of all a foreign funding agency, which is so tight and least wasteful.

3. As we have seen, OXFAM has spent a minimum of 6 per cent to a maximum of 17 per cent of its annual regional budget on small groups' activities. In a total of four years OXFAM has spent little more than 11 per cent of its budget on the small groups. I do not know how the rest of the 89 per cent of its western region budget was spent or what has been the impact of this budget. My guess is that what that 89 per cent has achieved is not anywhere near what has been achieved by the 11 per cent. What is difficult to understand is why

OXFAM's involvement in small groups has remained so low and why it has decreased in the last year.

4. In my view this small group phenomenon needs to be fully backed up and expanded. There are still many areas in Gujarat (the whole region of Saurashtra and Kutch, for instance, which has not been touched at all) where this programme needs to be extended. Whether OXFAM would like to get involved directly, or help such a programme through some other mode and medium, it may wish to decide depending on its own circumstances. I do see the possibility that with expansion, distortions may creep in. But even so I believe that this programme should be expanded. What is important is that the outside input of funds, monitoring and intervention should remain as careful and selective as it has been so far. This way distortions could be minimized.

5. As to existing groups, I think that there is a need for greater monitoring and intervention. I am quite nervous when I say this. For one thing, this might go against the grain: groups should be independent and self-reliant. Because the line between monitoring and control and intervention and domination are very thin, particularly with regard to these groups which are so fragile and may easily become dependent. Mistry has so far been able to steer a clear path between the two ends of the spectrum remarkably well. My feeling is that this is so not because of his skills, as because of his constant monitoring of and control over himself and his actions. And this comes perhaps because of his honesty and detachment regarding his own involvement rather than any training or experience. The intervenor would have to be very conscious and cautious. He would have to resist the temptation to 'lead' the groups. It would call for considerable self-restraint and detachment and yet great concern and involvement. I have ventured to suggest greater monitoring and intervention because I think that some groups would be helped a good deal with closer yet restrained attention from outside. For instance,

    a) A few groups seem to be stagnating. There are at least two cooperative societies—Vantda Milk Cooperative and the Vantda Bamboo Cooperative—which have potentialities. Their leaders have managed well. They

seem to be competent and enthusiastic and they have
generated considerable involvement of ordinary members. Yet they have not taken up any other activity.
With some more help and a little push these societies
may form new groups to take on developmental,
mobilizational and social action activities.

b) The Gambhoi Bamboo Workers' Cooperative has
been in existence for long but is barely surviving. It has
had very little impact on its members in economic or
social terms. Yet its very survival is itself an achievement because the Thuri community which it serves is
economically and socially very backward and the group
has hardly any literate member or leader. This group
would be benefited a lot if given greater attention and
support.

c) It is necessary for some of these groups to increase the
involvement of members of their groups and members
of their community. I do not mean simply participation
of the useful kind which is already there in some of the
groups. What I mean is a sense of involvement and
belonging. At present the groups are too leader oriented and leader dependant. This would perhaps always
remain so. But if a community as a whole is involved
with the group then the 'bad' leaders would be able to
do much less harm, and the chances of a group's stagnating or disintegrating be reduced.

d) It would also be helpful if records are kept in order and
reporting is done more regularly. While it is preferable
that groups not be burdened with paper work some
more formalization by way of systematic records and
regular reporting would instill a greater sense of ac-
countability.

e) Groups need to be helped to do some regular self-
assessment; a more conscious examination of the
implications of their decisions, activities and interaction with the outside world.

6. All this needs regular and frequent visits to the groups.
There are various modalities of doing this:

a) Core groups or some selected leaders of core groups
can do this.

b) District level unions of the groups can take up this responsibility.

c) An established voluntary agency can be funded to carry out this activity.

d) Some concerned individuals whose credentials are already known to OXFAM can be funded through a voluntary agency to undertake this activity.

e) OXFAM may directly employ two or three persons to do this work.

7. There are limitations in all these alternatives. I prefer the last two and particularly the last as being the least harmful. I shall not here expand on the role and modalities of persons so appointed by OXFAM. I am suggesting more monitoring by OXFAM because OXFAM has developed an approach and methodology of intervention which has enabled it to monitor but not control the groups. It is hoped that OXFAM's individualized approach would be institutionalized. I would suggest that OXFAM appoint a person in each district who, for want of any better name, could be called an Assistant Field Officer. He can function under the close guidance of the Field Officer. The idea can be first tried for a year with one person on a temporary basis.

8. I also see a clear need for OXFAM maintaining more systematic information and records about the groups. At present whatever information OXFAM's office has is inadequate and unorganized. I am aware that this would mean the expansion of OXFAM's office or administration. I fully appreciate and share the OXFAM culture of minimum administration and administrative expenses. Yet I suggest this because as the groups and areas expand such information would become necessary not only for determining responses to specific groups but for taking over-all strategic decisions. Initially, this could be tried out by getting part-time periodic or temporary help.

9. I would also suggest that now is the time for OXFAM to support some lateral organizations. By lateral organizations I do not mean organizations hierarchically linked with the small groups and giving them directions or funds. What I mean is a state-wide organization, composed of some leaders of these small groups and other activists in the region. Small

groups need legal, medical and sometimes political support and help from higher levels of politics and administration. The groups need to be related to broader issues, wider communities other than scheduled tribes, scheduled castes or rural poor (e.g., urban poor and minorities like Muslims), region-wide events (e.g., communal riots, anti-reservation agitation in Gujarat, Valia massacre, rehabilitation issues of the Narmada irrigation project). They need to interact with outside activists and voluntary organizations of different types and approach them more than they have been doing till now.

Equally important, the larger established voluntary agencies and activists need to be informed and educated about these small groups. They need to understand the successes, failures and limitations of these groups in their proper perspective.

In my few conversations with the higher order of outside activists about these groups I have found that their understanding of the phenomenon of small groups of weaker sections is limited and superfluous. They tend to assess and react to these groups from their own ideological perspectives. They either see them as immediate prospects for recruitment to larger revolutionary activities or as effective development agents influencing the government machinery for better and effective delivery of services. When they see some of these groups becoming stagnant or their leaders becoming corrupt or politically ambitious they get disappointed and tend to dismiss the groups as of not much consequence.

I have also observed among outside activists a tendency, as yet mild, to recruit some of the more capable leaders of these groups for their own activities; to try and pry them away from the mandals; to intervene in an intensive and detailed fashion; and attempt to guide and lead them.

In creating a lateral organization the various possibilities must be carefully considered. An existing organization could be brought in to do the job; a few people could be loosely brought together as a committee for a short duration on a trial basis; or a totally new organization could be formed. But whichever the method finally chosen, the organization should have a judicious mix of both outside activists and mandal leaders.